Copthorne Macdonald

TOWARD WISDOM

Finding Our Way to Inner Peace, Love & Happiness

HOUNSLOW

ISBN 0-88882-151-4

Publisher: Anthony Hawke
Editor: Shirley Knight Morris
Designer: Gerard Williams
Compositor: Robin Brass Studio
Printer: Best Gagné Book Manufacturers Inc.

Publication was assisted by
the Canada Council,
the Ontario Arts Council
and the Ontario Ministry of
Culture and Communications.

Hounslow Press
A Division of Anthony R. Hawke Limited
124 Parkview Avenue
Willowdale, Ontario, Canada
M2N 3Y5

Printed and bound in Canada

To all those positive influences along the way –
especially the first, Jane Copthorne Macdonald

Contents

Acknowledgements

Open Focus is a registered trademark of Biofeedback Computers Inc., Princeton New Jersey

The following source materials are gratefully acknowledged:

The Kenneth Rexroth quotes are from his article "William Golding," *The Atlantic Monthly,* Volume 215, No. 5, May, 1965.

The characteristics of self-actualizing people are from Abraham Maslow, *Toward a Psychology of Being,* Second Edition, New York: Van Nostrand Reinhold, 1968, p. 83.

Gregory Bateson's definition of information is from his book *Steps to an Ecology of Mind,* New York: Ballantine Books, 1972, p. 453.

Melvin Konner passages are from *The Tangled Wing,* New York: Holt, Rinehart & Winston, 1982.

The words of Albert Einstein are quoted in Joseph Goldstein, *The Experience of Insight: A Natural Unfolding,* Unity Press, Santa Cruz, 1976, p. 126.

The Alan Watts quotes in Chapters 4 and 7 are from *The Book: On the Taboo Against Knowing Who You Are,* New York: Vintage Press / Random House, 1972, pp. 8, 69.

Paul MacLean's comments appear in his paper "On the Evolution of Three Mentalities," *New Dimensions in Psychiatry: A World View,* Vol. 2, edited by Dr. Silvano Arieti and Dr. Gerard Chzanowki. New York: John Wiley and Sons, 1977, p. 325.

The Edward T. Hall passage from his book *Beyond Culture* is reproduced by permission of Bantam Doubleday Dell Publishing Group.

The Dalai Lama quotes are from Catherine Ingram's interview, "The Dalai Lama in Depth," *Yoga Journal,* Issue 90, Jan/Feb 1990.

Joseph Campbell passages are from *The Hero With a Thousand Faces,* Bollingen Series XVII. Copyright 1949 © renewed by Princeton University Press. Used with permission

Passages from *I AM THAT* are reproduced by permission of Chetana Pvt. Ltd., Bombay, India.

The Gail Sheehy quote is from her book *Passages,* New York: E.P. Dutton, 1974, 1976, p. 242.

The Aldous Huxley passage is from *The Perennial Philosophy,* London: Chatto & Windus, 1969, p. 38.

The definition of Open Focus is from the *Study Guide: Open Focus Cassette Training Series,* Basic 1000, Princeton, NJ: Biofeedback Computers, 1977.

Alan Watts quotes Oscar Wilde in *The Meaning of Happiness: The Quest for Freedom of the Spirit in Modern Psychology and the Wisdom of the East,* New York: Harper Colophon Books, 1969 (1940), p. 40

Da Free John's comments are from *The Bodily Location of Happiness,* Clearlake, CA: Dawn Horse Press, 1982.

The E.F. Schumacher quote is from *A Guide for the Perplexed.* New York: Harper and Row. 1977. p. 39

Edward Hoffman quotes Abraham Maslow in *The Right to be Human: A Biography of Abraham Maslow,* Los Angeles: Jeremy P. Tarcher, 1988, p. 298.

The T. S. Eliot line is from his poem "Burnt Norton," *Four Quartets,* London: Faber and Faber, 1959 (1944), p. 15.

The Tony Bastick quote is from his book *Intuition: How We Think and Act,* Chichester: John Wiley & Sons, 1982, p. 277.

The Virginia Burden Tower quote is from her book *The Process of Intuition,* 2nd Ed., Wheaton, Ill.: The Theosophical Publishing House, 1987, p. 83.

Philip Goldberg passages are from *The Intuitive Edge,* Los Angeles: Jeremy P. Tarcher, Inc., 1983.

ACKNOWLEDGEMENTS

The Hazel Barnes quote is from her book *Humanistic Existentialism*.

The Arthur Koestler quote is from his book *The Act of Creation*, New York: Dell Publishing Co., 1964, 1967, p. 633.

The Goethe quote is from *Goethe's World View*, Ed. by Frederick Unger, Tr. by Heinz Norden, New York: Frederick Unger Publishing Co., 1963, p. 141.

The Ranier Maria Rilke quote is from *Letters to a Young Poet*, New York: W.W. Norton, 1934, 1954, 1962, p. 59.

The list of Vipassana sitting groups is from *Inquiring Mind: A Semi-annual Journal of the Vipassana Community.*

Preface

This book is about wisdom and the process of becoming wise. It has its roots in two major turning points in my life. The first dates back 25 years, to a time when I was just leaving my 20s and entering my 30s. I was, in those days, a corporate design engineer and engineering manager with a very narrow outlook on life. I cringe as I recall my self-assured smugness, the absolute confidence I had that technology was the centre of all that mattered. I saw everything else as some kind of frill, as some variety of missing the mark. Kenneth Rexroth recognized me and my kind; he called us the "technical intelligentsia." He also called us "Neanderthals with slide rules."

A corporate management seminar was the unlikely place where the first seeds of change were planted. It was there that I was introduced to Abraham Maslow's theory of motivation and psychological growth. I found Maslow's concept of self-actualization exciting, and for the next decade the idea of "becoming all I'm capable of becoming" was the focus of my life.

I spent that decade, my 30s, discovering, adventuring, and watching my outlook broaden. I began with a year of intensive reading (Camus, Sartre, Kazantzakis, Hesse, Maslow, and others) and then began a series of outward-oriented adventures. Electronic art was the first exploration; that was followed by three years in Manhattan as Director of Research for a small electronics company. Next came a 13-month backpack trip around the world. During that trip the foreignness of other places and people vanished, and I developed concerns about third world problems and the well-being of our planet. These concerns led to involvement in the alternatives movement of the '70s, writing magazine articles and columns, and changing countries. At the end of the decade I heeded the advice of both feminism and brain-hemisphere theory and took steps to develop the nurturing side of myself. I worked awhile as a hospital orderly, and then with the elderly.

The second turning point came at age 41 when I attended a 12-day meditation retreat and my mind became still and quiet for the first time in my adult life. When I left that retreat the world was the same old world, but my way of looking at it had changed profoundly. I had begun an inward-oriented adventure. The investigation prompted by that first retreat occupied much of the next 15 years – and still continues. During those years I read hundreds of books and scientific articles, and spent several thousand hours doing various types of meditative practice. The goal of both endeavors was to arrive at satisfying answers to some fundamental questions: "What is going on?" "What's it all about?" and "What am I to do about it?" The search was always for explanations that rang true both intuitively *and* intellectually. In a sense, this book is a status report on the investigation to date.

The book began to take form when I started to see my quarter century of adventure, experience, and insight in the context of wisdom and the growth of wisdom. For one thing, I realized that whole-person development was one of the keys to becoming wise: development of both intellect *and* intuition, analysis *and* synthesis, left brain hemisphere *and* right. For another, I realized that many facets of the world problematique – biosphere degradation, resource depletion, and the continuing follies of war and terrorism – could be attributed to a serious lack of wisdom on the part of both power-wielders and ordinary folk.

Many of us are knowledgeable, but few of us are wise. During this century, industrial society helped us become the most knowledgeable populace in history. Some of us applied our knowledge to the creation of powerful technologies. All of us have used those technologies to create comfortable lives for ourselves. Our intentions were usually honourable in all this, but our actions much of the time were not guided by that holistic, value-connected kind of understanding called wisdom.

The situation the world faces today is incredibly complex. Long-cherished values have begun to conflict with each other: material comfort vs. an uncontaminated world; economic growth now vs. economic well-being for our grandchildren. And things just seem to get worse. *Toward Wisdom* takes the position that applied wisdom is the only effective way to deal with our personal/global problematique. Wisdom is no longer an option or a frill. We, and the world, need wisdom-based analyses of our problems followed by wisdom-based action. Before wisdom can take control of the situation, however, large numbers of people must become wise. Can this be brought about? How?

In the past, becoming wise was left to chance; a few people became wise before they died, but most did not. If wisdom really is the only way out of our global mess, then this lackadaisical approach will no longer do. Fortunately, today we know more than ever before about what wisdom is and what prevents people from becoming wise. We also know that just as we can become knowledgeable by going through a sometimes arduous but well-defined process, so we can become wise by going through a different kind of arduous process.

On the bright side, we see the amazing power of individual wise people to change things for the better. Their accomplishments are all out of proportion to their numbers. Consider the best of each year's nominees for the Nobel Peace Prize, for instance. What would our world be like if there were millions more with their dedication, skills, and wise perspectives on life? Yes, becoming wise is likely to take as much effort as becoming knowledgeable – but is there anything more worthwhile? Do we, in fact, have any other choice?

The first chapter of *Toward Wisdom* explores the nature of wisdom. The next three examine impediments to wisdom – those things that make it difficult to adopt wise ways of seeing and functioning. We look at what those obstacles are, how they work, and how they came to be. Chapter 5 points out that we've been mucking up our world, and makes the case that we need to get past those impediments and become wise. The next five chapters (six through 10) discuss practical ways of doing just that. Chapter 11 is about freedom, choice, and responsibility; 12 deals with wisdom in relationships; and 13 with creating a wisdom-based culture. In the final chapter I comment on books that I have found particularly helpful, and tell how to access other wisdom-fostering resources.

1

What Is Wisdom?

Wisdom is not one thing; it is a whole array of better-than-ordinary ways of being, and living, and dealing with the world. Because of this, and because individual wise people express wisdom's characteristics in different ways and to different degrees, this chapter's question has no brief answer.

Short statements about wisdom can be helpful as long as we realize that each expresses only part of the truth. We could say, for example, that wisdom involves:

seeing things clearly; seeing things as they are

acting in prudent and effective ways

acting with the well-being of the whole in mind

deeply understanding the human/cosmic situation

knowing when to act and when not to act

being able to handle whatever arises with peace of mind and an effective, compassionate, holistic response

being able to anticipate potential problems and avoid them

Each statement helps clarify some aspect of wisdom, but none tells the whole story.

The self-actualizing and ego-transcending people that Abraham Maslow studied were wise people, and Maslow's writings tell us much about the nature of wisdom. Maslow's self-actualizers focused on concerns outside of themselves; they liked solitude and privacy more than the average person, and they tended to be more detached than ordinary from the dictates and expectations of their culture. They were inner-directed people. They were creative, too, and appreciated the world around them with a sense of awe and wonder. In love relationships they respected the other's individuality and felt joy at the other's successes. They gave more love than most people, and needed less. Central to their lives was a set of values that Maslow called the Being-Values, or B-Values: wholeness, perfection, completion, justice, aliveness, richness, simplicity, beauty, goodness, uniqueness, effortlessness, playfulness, truth, honesty, reality, self-sufficiency.[1]

The inner directedness that Maslow noted is a key feature of wisdom. It arises, in part, from acquiring new, more helpful perspectives. We live today in a swirl of information, and we need some of this raw data to arrive at the answers we seek. Knowledge, however, is *interpreted* data. If the perspective or conceptual model through which we interpret our data is inappropriate, or flawed, then our knowledge is flawed and will lead us astray. For many people, the task of becoming wise is not one of absorbing more information, more raw facts; it is to put the significant facts they already have into appropriate contexts, to view them from more helpful perspectives.

In later chapters I will attempt to show that we human beings acquired certain perspectives from evolution and culture which are, in fact, flawed perspectives – perspectives that limit and distort our understanding of reality. Certain biology-based perspectives, for example, arose to aid personal and species survival in more trying, more primitive times. Today they impede our movement toward a global kind of understanding; they impede our movement toward wisdom.

Certain culture-based perspectives also stand in our way. Our industrial culture – in actualizing its values, in looking out for its interests – has indoctrinated us with interpretive frameworks that reflect and promote those values and interests. It has passed on to us a set of approved ways of looking at things and has said, "Look at the data of life from these vantage points; interpret your facts according to these guidelines." There is nothing unusual about this; all cultures do it. But cultural institutions that prompt us to see the world from a having, desiring, possessing, consuming perspective aren't leading us in the direction of wisdom, inner peace, and deeply-felt contentment. Becoming wise requires that we adopt other perspectives, other interpretive frameworks – ones that do reveal truth and encourage movement toward holistic understanding and widespread well-being.

The words of the great spiritual teachers have added much to our understanding of wisdom. So have the writing and thinking of the wisest of the world's leaders: Jefferson, Lincoln, and Gandhi, for example, and more recently, Gro Bruntland and Vaclav Havel. Writers of serious literature helped by giving us literary role models – wise people, and people in the process of becoming wise – Lawrence Durrell's *Clea*, for example, Herman Hesse's *Demian*, Nikos Kazantzakis's *Zorba* – and Kazantzakis himself in *Report to Greco*. Reading books by and about wise people can help us grasp the multi-faceted nature of wisdom. Here, however, let us focus on a few specifics. Let's look at five frequently-encountered attributes of wisdom – five characteristics that appear to have special importance to us, the people of earth, in this last decade of the twentieth century.

A reality-seeking attitude

Wisdom, maturity, and happiness seem to go hand in hand with figuring out how life and the world work – with discovering the nature of the rules, laws, and programming that dictate what will happen under what conditions. Wise people know that the more deeply and accurately they come to understand key processes within and without, the better able they are to live their personal lives in harmony with what is happening moment-to-moment. Wise people want to find out. Wise people are reality seekers.

Developing an accurate, comprehensive picture of reality does not happen easily. We arrive on earth having to play the game of existence but not knowing the rules or even the object of the game. Then, gradually, each of us builds a worldview – a mental map of how it all is and what it's all about. The maps made by wise people are in many respects more complete and more accurate than the maps made by others, but for even the wisest, their picture of how it all is never becomes much more than a rough sketch. Despite talk about "fully enlightened beings," I strongly suspect that no one has ever been completely out of the dark.

Almost by definition, reality seekers remain open-minded, flexible, and receptive. They know that all explanations, models, and metaphors are just pointers to truth and crude maps of reality. All are approximate and partial. Further refinement of the maps is always in order. And since wise people are not ego-attached to their present views, when they do get new data, or flip to a new perspective, their worldviews and explanatory words change.

Spiritual teachers have created cosmologies, psychologies, and ethical systems. Many of their psychologies are similar. So-called mystical experiences are largely independent of specific information; thus, they tend to be similar for everyone who has them. It is because of this that the perennial philosophy is perennial, and independent of culture and geography. People who have seen the world from a *perennial philosophy* perspective recognize the reports of others who have done so. There is agreement.

Cosmologies, on the other hand, tend to differ widely – leading me to suspect that they are based, at least in part, on culturally-acquired information. If Gautama the Buddha lived today I suspect that his psychology would not be much different, but that his cosmology would be.

Imagine that the great reality seekers of ancient times – people like Jesus and Gautama – had continued to live on through the centuries. Do you share my guess that they would have made the transition into the present smoothly and organically – excited about each breakthrough in knowledge along the way, each widening and refining of their views? The Great Ones had to be open-minded reality-seekers. It is their followers who have sometimes become closed and rigid – true believers – guardians of temple and church who took each word of their leaders to be absolute truth. *Words aren't truth.* Wise people recognize this; they remain seekers rather than becoming believers.

A reality-seeking attitude can also help us find ethical and moral truth. Many wise people of the past – spiritual leaders, philosophers, and great writers – observed what works in human society, and what doesn't. Over the centuries their observations have been shared with an ever larger audience, yet their advice is largely ignored by each new generation. Moses was one of those wise people. Now, at this point in my life, I think that his Ten Commandments are a pretty good set of guidelines for living. Nevertheless, since first hearing about them at age five or six I have lied, stolen, dishonoured my father and my mother, committed adultery, and more. We seem to find it very difficult to take someone else's word on ethical matters. We feel the need to explore life's limits for ourselves and come to our own conclusions.

I don't think our distrust of do-what-I-say ethics will fundamentally change, and that's okay. We don't need new lists of do's and don'ts. We don't need new codes of conduct. They wouldn't really help. What does help is a reality-seeking attitude toward our own experience. "Why do my relationships fall apart?" "Why do I keep getting myself into this kind of mess?" "What is reality telling me?" "What is the lesson in this?" "Is there a general rule of the Game that I've missed up to now?" Wise people ask themselves these kinds of questions, and when they do, the answers come. Wise people are attentive people, and their attention to what is not working well eventually leads to greater harmony. They know that the solution to a problem almost always lies in a clear understanding of the problem itself.

Staying open is often uncomfortable. The pain of uncertainty, of growing, comes with the territory of human existence. A certain directivity toward perfection may well be built into the cosmic process and, as Maslow's research indicated, into each person. But the means to actualize perfection are not ideal. Some degree of discomfort appears to be the price of continual transcendence, continual replacement of old ways of seeing with new ways.

Non-reactive acceptance

As we will see in Chapter 2, part of evolution's legacy to the human species is the mammalian brain structure called *the limbic system* and the palette of intense, reactive emotions associated with it. These strong emotions – fear, anger, lust, hatred, greed, craving, jealousy, envy, etc. – are the cause of much human suffering. The person experiencing these forms of emotional reactivity suffers, and if reactive emotions take control of our behaviour, others are often made to suffer too.

Wise people have learned how to deal with reactive impulses so they don't become prolonged reactive states of mind, and so they don't result in reactive behaviour. Wise people don't rail against the present moment's informational content. They know that by the time we become aware of this moment's event, it has already taken place. Accepting it is therefore the only sane, rational response. It's not that wise people avoid acting. In the moment that follows they may very well choose to act. But their actions are almost always guided by wiser centres of control; their actions are not knee-jerk responses to impulses from the limbic brain.

For the most part, wise people live non-reactively. They live the present moment from a centre of awareness, acceptance, energy, basic goodness, and quiet joy. They know that when fear is dropped, courage fills the mind. They know that when anger and hate are dropped, compassion is there. They know that when wanting and greed are dropped, mental peace, primal happiness, and equanimity will be present.

Holistic seeing

The attention and energy of most people is focused on their immediate situation. The intensity of their concern about other situations, people, and events drops rapidly as those things become more distant in space, time, and relationship. The concerns of wise people, on the other hand, go far beyond the immediate and the personal. They have acquired a variety of perspectives that I lump together under the umbrella phrase *holistic seeing*.

Many of these holistic perspectives are intellectual ones. An understanding of concepts like **system**, **evolution**, and **problematique**, for instance, can help us appreciate complexity, interconnectedness, and wholeness. When deeply understood, such concepts lead to more expansive, more holistic kinds of thinking. Let's touch briefly on the three I just mentioned.

A **system** is a whole that consists of interacting and interdependent components in a persisting pattern of relationship. The human body/mind is a system. The universe is a system. A TV set is a system. The relationships that define a system may involve events, or spatial configurations, or both. System *components* frequently capture our attention; we can see them directly. Unfortunately, system *relationships* tend not to be as flashy and grabby as the components. In some cases they do not give rise to sensory messages at all, and may totally escape our notice. To understand what is really going on in a system it is often helpful to create a visual model of the relationships involved. We can look carefully at a radio's innards, for example – perhaps even name and count all the various parts – but unless we are familiar with what each component is capable of doing, and can visualize the complex way in which they are interconnected, we won't know how or why that radio works.

People who have thoroughly internalized the **system** concept realize that the bits and pieces around us don't tell the whole story. These people know that to really understand what is going on you must also come to grips with the pattern of relationships that exists between and among those bits and pieces.

Evolution, in the most complete sense of that term, is the "complexification" of the universe, a process of system building and information creating that has been going on since the Big Bang at t = 0, about 15 billion years ago. Using Jacques Monod's terms **chance** and **necessity**, we could say that evolution is driven by necessity, and its details are elaborated by chance. Necessity, in this case, is the entire ensemble of natural laws, working together. Chance is sometimes absolute randomness, as in quantum processes. It is also the unexpected and unpredictable that occurs when highly-independent chains of cause and effect intersect: Two people, living their individual lives, are invited to the same party. A meteor, travelling through the universe on one trajectory, strikes the earth, traveling through the universe on another. One of a hundred million sperm wins a race, enters an egg, and combines its genes with that egg's genes.

Without a grasp of evolutionary processes we have little sense of our deep kinship with the universe. In addition, we fail to sense the role that we humans are now playing as active agents of evolution.

Behind the uncommon term **problematique** lies a powerful perspective. I first encountered it in the 1972 Club of Rome report, *Limits to Growth,* and it changed forever the way I look at global difficulties. The idea behind the term is this: The world's people do not face a basketful of separate problems. The world's major problems – population growth, environmental degradation, resource depletion, etc. – are so intimately linked that they are best thought of as facets of a single overarching problem, a **problematique.** To avoid making other aspects of the problematique worse, our problem-solving must be done with all of it in mind – not just the particular aspect that happens to occupy centre stage at the moment.

Realization of oneness

For a long time now there have been small groups of people who saw some form of unity that most others could not see – or at least could not internalize to the point where it motivated their actions. Several of these unitive perspectives relate to the world of form and function; one is rooted in Being itself.

Among the information-based, form-and-function unities is the unity of human psychology. I experience fear, and hatred, and jealousy. So does every other human being. Seeing this can eventually lead to a unity of compassionate understanding. Our unskilfulness and outdated programming unite us – as does our potential for wisdom.

The evolutionary view of what is going on in the universe points to another form-and-function unity: the unity of process, a unity based on the physical interdependence that permeates the entire cosmos. In this view the whole universal process is one entity. We humans are localized, aware nodes of that process. My physical body is not a process unto itself, a closed system; it is an open system, an intrinsic part of a much larger physical process. It is a subsystem in a process that includes the biosphere, the sun, and in fact, the entire universe. This is a solid tangible unity based on the physical reality of our existence.

Then there is the unity of biological kinship. Not only do all humans belong to one species, but we are in some sense related to every other living thing. The twist of all DNA is in the same direction – one of two equally possible directions. This indicates to many scientists that all plant and animal species descended from a single early cell. Then too, the chemistry of all life forms is the same. Every organism in the diverse biological world was constructed using just a few standard chemical building blocks.

Some of the wisest people have seen a primal Being-based unity. This unity is the unity that the perennial philosophy would have us see, the unity dealt with in the mystical traditions of both East and West, the unity of transcendence, of Maslow's "Farther Reaches." It is an intuition-based type of holistic seeing. Coming to see this unity requires an intuitive shift of vantage point – and ultimately, of identification. The world observed by these people is the same world that everyone else sees; nothing external has changed. But they suddenly see that reality in a new context; they see in the data of life a meaning that wasn't evident before.

Involved here is what we might call an intuitive version of the perceptual *gestalt flip*. The gestalts that most psychology books discuss are visual gestalts. We might look at a set of black marks on white paper and say, "That's a face." It's not really a face, of course, but our brain has conjured up a "face" gestalt from the arrangement of marks. Or, as usually happens when we look out the window, we attend to our visual field not as single field of varying colour and light intensity, but as a collection of gestalts, a collection of separate "things."

We're all familiar with drawings of objects that can be seen in more than one way. I recall one such drawing. At first glance I abstracted from it subjective reality number one: an attractive young woman seated at a dressing table, looking at herself in the mirror. Then my perception did a flip, and I saw the same pattern of black marks on the paper as the image of a skull: subjective reality number two. Which subjective reality truly represented the objective reality? Both did, but each was an incomplete representation. The drawing itself, the objective reality, contained both a skull aspect and a seated woman aspect. Both of the conscious experiences were valid, accurate, but incomplete analogs of the objective reality, the drawing itself. Most introductory psychology texts include drawings that produce this gestalt-flip phenomenon. Typical pictures are a vase that can also be seen as two faces, a stairway that can be seen as a ceiling cornice, and a young woman that flips to an old woman. Each is a drawing that can be viewed in two completely different and mutually exclusive ways.

The point here is that it is possible to have gestalt flips of conception and intuition as well as perception. Profound insights often involve a flip from one conceptual interpretation to another, or one intuitive sense of things to another. The old way of seeing the reality is still an option – and perhaps valid for certain purposes. But there is now a second way. It was always there. Others had seen it, and might have told us about it – but we hadn't seen it for ourselves. Then one day, FLIP. In a fraction of a second, we switch perspectives. We find ourselves still looking at the same old data, but we now see those data in a dramatically different way. We experience another valid – and sometimes more significant – way of understanding what *is*.

People who have flipped to the universal-wisdom or perennial-philosophy perspective report that existence involves two different kinds of reality. One is a transient, fragmented, surface reality which most of us mistakenly take to be THE reality. The other is an eternal, enabling oneness which these people realize is our true nature and identity – our deepest, truest Self. For millennia, insightful people have been beating about the bush of Truth, trying to express this realization clearly in words. Here, in the paragraphs that follow, I will attempt to do that once again – this time using language, concepts, and metaphors of our present "information age."

Psychologist Maslow referred to Being, but in doing so he was an exception among scientists. Being is not something that scientists normally talk about. Scientists talk about phenomena. It is philosophers and spiritual teachers who have talked about Being. The ancients spoke of Being and Existence, Essence and Form, the Unconditioned and the Conditioned, Spirit and Manifestation. Later, Kant spoke of Noumenon and Phenomenon in a similar way. The general sense of those who used these terms was that Being/Essence/the Unconditioned/Spirit/Noumenon was ungraspable but eternal, primary yet unknowable. It was the Real. In contrast, Existence/Form/the Conditioned/Manifestation/Phenomena was knowable yet transient, ephemeral – even illusory. It was the Unreal.

When I first encountered this sort of thinking, years ago, I brushed it aside as irrelevant metaphysical hogwash. What could be more real than phenomena? Later, when I began to find science's answers less than complete, I asked myself why these two groups of serious, sincere people were talking past each other. Sages and philosophers, after all, are reality seekers. Scientists are reality seekers too. Both groups are interested in what *is*, and both groups comment on it – yet the two groups have historically described the same reality differently. Why is that?

The reason eventually dawned on me: science and philosophy approach reality with different aims, and with different questions in mind. The two groups do deal with the same reality, but they don't get the same answers because they don't ask the same questions. They subject the data to different interpretive frameworks, and this results in different – though not necessarily incompatible – descriptions of reality.

Our modern-day concepts of *medium* and *message* helped to clarify the situation for me. Science has declared its chief interest to be the study of physical phenomena, and these phenomena involve both a permanent medium-like aspect and a transient message-like aspect. The medium is energy. The message is the space-time patterning of that energy – its informational configuration as specific forms of energy, varieties of matter,[2] and the relationship of these to each other. For most scientific purposes nothing would be gained by splitting a phenomenon into its medium and message aspects. It would not help answer scientific questions. It would have no explanatory value within that context.

The philosopher and the spiritual seer occupy the same world of phenomena in which the scientist lives, but they do find value in making a distinction between phenomena's temporary and permanent aspects. Seeing that phenomena have both an eternal "medium" aspect and a transient "message" aspect does have explanatory value within a philosophical/spiritual context. This perspective gives better answers to questions that involve meaning, and it illuminates the eternal. It gives us a view that takes us beyond the usual scientific view without in any way negating it. From the medium-message perspective, scientific truth and philosophical or spiritual truth are seen to be non-conflicting subsets of a more complete *Truth*.

The medium/message model also applies to mental reality. Here, the underlying medium is pure awareness, sentience, subjectivity, the ground of mind.[3] The mental message is mind content in its many forms – thoughts, feelings, perceptions, imaginings – all of them being informational modulations of awareness, modulations created in human beings by the patterned firing of brain neurons.

Concepts like medium, message, and information – as they are currently understood – were not common currency even a few decades ago, let alone in ancient times. In the past, words like *Being, essence, Spirit,* and *form* were the best terms available for getting an intellectual grip on the perennial-philosophy view of reality. Today, the new terms and concepts enable those who understand them to get even closer to the heart of the perennial-philosophy view. The information-age explanation goes like this:

> Existence involves the interpenetration and interaction of three strata, or realms, or types of reality: energy, awareness, and information. Energy and awareness are media. (Or more probably, two aspects of one medium.) Information is message. Energy and awareness are the grounds from which existence springs (the paint and canvas). Information is the content (the brush strokes, the emerging pattern). Energy is the eternal ground of all physical existence and the active principle behind all change. Awareness is the ground of all mental existence. Information is the evanescent, space-based, time-based, always-changing overlay which – as form and content for the other two – creates the mental/physical drama of existence.

> Pure, formless energy is the cosmic modelling clay – the medium which is overlaid with informational patterns, with form, to become the objective universe.

> Pure, contentless awareness is the medium of subjective experience. It interfaces with informational patterns of energy difference that wave or

modulate awareness, creating mind content and the phenomenon we call mind.

Information – form, pattern, difference – is that third element. Information is the abstract organizing matrix that lies at the root of any expression, in any medium. It is the organizing principle embodied in the blueprint of a building and in the building itself. It is the sameness to be found in a book written in English and in its French translation.

In information theory this abstract organizing matrix is seen to be a matrix of differences. Gregory Bateson defined the elementary unit of information as "a difference which makes a difference. . ." Information is the array of significant differences that defines form. Differences in position. Differences in time. Differences in colour, intensity, pressure, texture. Differences of any kind signify information.

Information is knowledge in the abstract, disembodied knowledge. It is there in the concept, and the physical structure that embodies the concept. It is there in the motion, and in the equations that describe that motion. The same information exists in the imagination of the composer, the musical score, the performance, the wavy groove of the vinyl record, the electrical signal going to the loudspeaker, the sound in the room, the vibrations of the eardrum, the pattern of neuronal firings in the brain, and the subjective perception of the sound.

The universe is a display, a composition, a work, wrought in the primary media of expression. It is an ongoing "media event": an ever-changing in-form-ation and re-form-ation of energy – exhibiting and enjoying a vast variety of phenomena, effects and characteristics.

From the standpoint of energy, the universe is a giant physical process – a system of systems, a megasystem or suprasystem. From the standpoint of awareness, it is a mosaic of thought processes – a megathought or suprathought. From either standpoint it is an informational construct – a moulding, a forming, a dynamic patterning of the two-faceted ground of being: Energy-Awareness.[4]

It would be foolish to deny the reality of our physical existence, or call it an illusion. But there is a difference between the reality of form and specific function, and the reality of the underlying interpenetrating ground of being that makes form and function possible. I might give you a lump of modelling clay having some shape and ask: "Which is real, the clay or its shape?" The reality of the shape exists until you squish the thing in your hands and make another shape. But the reality of the clay itself remains unchanged. The perennial philosophy view holds that our true Self and Being inheres in the cosmic modelling clay. The body/mind's earthly existence inheres in the temporary shape – the temporary systemic pattern – into which the clay has been moulded.

Cosmic modelling clay is more sophisticated, of course, than the stuff kids play with. It is energized, and can mould itself. In that respect it is more like yeasty bread dough than passive clay. The yeast within a lump of dough is active. In creating bubbles of gas it gives microscopic texture and macroscopic form to the loaf. The dough, in rising and baking, develops an intricate informational structure. The original dough is still there, but no longer as a homogeneous lump. The dough's active principle – the yeast – has been at work creating an informational labyrinth. The only *physical* reality is still the dough, but an *informational* reality has also come into existence: the bread's texture and overall shape. The universe behaves similarly as it evolves. Guided by the entire matrix of natural law, the universe – like a giant lump of rising dough – acquires form.

Being, however, is more than just its energy and awareness aspects. It is also the realm of potential and potential-actualizing process. It is the pregnant Void – void of form or information – but the source of all form, capability, and wisdom. Being has the potential to clothe itself in a bewildering variety of informational patterns. And the universe is rigged so that this will happen. The cosmic algorithms that define the laws of nature work together to actualize potentials whenever they can be actualized. This results in a general tendency for something to happen rather than nothing. The universe has a built in YES! It is intrinsically adventurous. Energy says YES and *does*. Awareness says YES and *experiences*.

Those who deeply internalize the perennial philosophy perspective experience a shift in identification. Their former primary identification as a person is replaced by a new primary identification as Being itself. Identification as a person remains an option, and is useful in everyday circumstances, but they can flip to their new vantage point at will. From that vantage point they see themselves as Being. To use my terminology, they see themselves as energy acting to uplevel the informational process, and awareness enjoying the perception of it.

Making this shift of identification does not happen easily. Although we are surrounded by evidence of the unity, very few are ready to see it. Our biocomputer/brains are currently programmed to believe in a personal self, and our whole personal-survival pleasure-seeking orientation comes out of that belief. Gut-level acceptance of oneness means gut-level disidentification with a small-s self – and most people are not ready for that. In later chapters we will explore this identification issue more deeply.

Behaviour that benefits others

Wise people live their daily lives in accord with wise perspectives and wise values. As a result, their actions make the world around them a better place. They help others to grow. They live compassionately. They resolve conflicts and in other ways maximize harmony and general well-being. If their own growth in wisdom is carried to the point where identification with Being takes place, they stop differentiating between themselves, the universe, and what needs to be done. At that point they see themselves and the rest of humanity as Being itself – evolving, and living progressively higher values.

As Maslow pointed out, when you see clearly what is, you automatically know what to do. Reality, in other words, has its own ethical imperatives. These ethical "musts" become obvious when the mind becomes quiet – when the clear truth about what needs to be done is not obscured by personal wants, fears, and dislikes. Wise people are able to sense ethical imperatives and act on them because intuition and intellect – working as co-ordinated partners – now run the show. What to do becomes clear under these conditions. So does what not to do. Wise people not only work to uplevel the process, they refuse to commit their time and energy to the unhelpful.

CHAPTER

2

Emotion-Based Reactivity

The more I learned about the nature of wisdom and wise people, the more certain I was that this was the kind of person I wanted to be. But how was I going to accomplish this?

Many questions arose. Why wasn't I wise already? What held me back? What did I need to do differently? Determined to find answers, I began to read about brain and mind function, and to watch the way my own mind worked. I eventually began to see what stood between me and wisdom. The myriad specifics were, for the most part, instances of three general kinds of obstacle:

1. Emotion-based reactivity – various forms of wanting what you don't have and wanting to get rid of what you do have,

2. Ignorance – missing or erroneous information, and

3. Delusion – the inappropriate interpretation of valid information.

In this chapter we will consider the first of these hindrances: mind states and actions that are dominated by "heavy," reactive emotions.

The human brain/mind is an amazing complex of integrated structures and physical/mental functions that we are just beginning to understand. In the view of most scientists, it evolved to enhance the ability of human beings to survive and reproduce. Remarkably, the brain that evolution developed to meet those primal needs turned out to be a general-purpose multi-function system with potentials that go far beyond personal and species survival. Each individual brain/mind comes into the world with the biological base that evolution created and a large array of undeveloped potentials. Once here, it develops in response to local circumstances. The milieu in which it matures determines which of its many potentials will be actualized.

Sensitivity to the environment and the ability to respond to environmental change arose early in the evolution of living things. One familiar example is the ability of plants to shift position to maximize their exposure to light. Time-lapse photography reveals that some plants actually follow the sun, changing position continuously during the course of a day. These plant responses and the responses of the least complex forms of animal life appear to many scientists to arise from totally physical, reflex-like mechanisms. They feel that mentality plays no active part in these processes.

As evolution progressed, more-complex forms of animal life emerged. New physical systems appeared, and older systems were modified. Changes that resulted in survival or reproduction advantages were passed on to offspring and became features of those species and descendent ones. Eventually, beings evolved that could see, taste, smell, and hear. And beings evolved that could move about in their environment and manipulate it in sophisticated ways.

It was during this period of emerging complexity that mentality began to find its niche. The physical-only, reflexive, stimulus-response approach might have worked well in simple situations. But complex organisms were equipped to receive several different kinds of sensory information simultaneously, and to respond in a variety of ways. If each separate subsystem had acted independently, behavioural chaos or gridlock might have resulted. To avoid this sort of problem, analysis and decision-making systems evolved – systems in which mentality plays a functional role. The implication seems to be that in complex situations, mental evaluation and decision-making is a simpler and more efficient evolutionary solution than physical-only solutions. In any event, it is the route that evolution took.

Some scientists assume that this transition to mental evaluation and control took place when mammals evolved. Others assume that it happened much earlier, or was not a sharp transition at all. One scientist expressed his feeling that frogs (a step or two below the reptiles on evolution's phylogenetic ladder) operate in the reflex mode. They appear to capture passing insects and jump to avoid danger in an automatic, mindless fashion. When this scientist looked at a lizard, however, he saw curiosity and other evidence of a mind at work. There is much speculation, but no one yet knows for sure. When scientists better understand the difference between mentality-supporting brain structures and strictly physical ones, we will have a much clearer idea.

It turns out that the reptilian brain and the early mammalian brain both represent significant milestones in evolution. They are in fact still with us, in pretty much their original forms, within our human brains. The human brain, we are told, is not a single brain at all. Inside our skulls are three separate (but interconnected) brains, one nested inside another.

The reptilian brain is the oldest and most primitive of the three. It originated with the reptiles and is the only brain that a reptile has. As evolution progressed, this reptilian brain was not abandoned or drastically modified. It remained, doing much the same job for birds, small mammals and humans that it did for snakes, lizards, and alligators. In a human head this reptilian brain is the innermost of the three nested brains. It is sometimes called the brain stem, and consists of the medulla, pons, and midbrain.

When mammals emerged, evolution simply capped the reptilian brain with another one. This cap, this old mammalian brain, is called the limbic system. It surrounds the reptilian brain and consists of the hypothalamus, pituitary, hippocampus, amygdala, and fornix.

In recently-evolved mammals, the old mammalian brain is surrounded by a third brain, the neocortex. In human heads it is this neocortex that deals with language, visualization, evaluation, problem-solving, and reflective decision-making.

Paul D. MacLean, who originated this *Triune Brain* theory, considered each of the three sub-brains to be a biological computer — each with its own special form of subjectivity and intelligence. His research indicated that the reptilian brain is the home of primal animalistic behaviours such as selecting homesites, establishing territory, displaying to enemies and potential mates, hunting, mating, breeding, imprinting, forming social hierarchies and selecting leaders. MacLean felt that even in human beings these functions have their roots in the hard-wired ancestral memories of the reptilian brain.

The strong reactive emotions connected with individual and species survival appear to originate in the limbic system. Oral and sexual pleasure (and behaviour) arise when certain parts of the limbic system are electrically stimulated. Fear, anger, and hostile behaviour arise when other parts are stimulated. This development of strong, reactive emotion was another of evolution's master strokes: Increase the chances of survival by creating highly intense subjective experiences that shock the animal into a state of alertness, ready it to take remedial action, and give it a strong general indication of what kind of action to take.

The neocortex consists of two hemispheric sub-brains connected by a band of nerve fibres called the corpus callosum. A lot has been written about what activities go on in these two cortical hemispheres – much of it oversimplified, and some of it conflicting. Most commentators have associated the left hemisphere with analytical, verbal, linear, and intellectual thought processes. They have associated the right with holistic, spatial, non-linear, and intuitive processes. Recent research indicates that the left does seem more involved with detail and sequence, the right more with pattern and simultaneity, but that the hemispheres are less specialized than was first thought. Also, in normal people (those of us with an intact corpus callosum), the two hemispheres almost always work together.

The neocortex has several areas devoted to specific, well-defined functions. There is the *somatosensory area* that processes touch and other body sensations, the *motor area* that controls the movement of various body parts, the *auditory cortex* that processes auditory information, and the *visual cortex* that processes visual information. Those areas of the neocortex that are not sensory or motor areas are called *association areas*. These areas are involved in neural circuits with other brain structures, and take part in many information processing activities.

The brain's most advanced association area is the *frontal cortex* located just behind the forehead. It is in this brain area where planning and decision-making take place. Being richly supplied with neural connections to the limbic system, it also serves as the "report and control centre for the emotions." Speech control (left hemisphere) and pattern recognition (right hemisphere) occur here, too.

Although some functions can be localized to specific areas of the brain, many functions (such as memory) cannot. Because of this, there has been an increasing appreciation of the importance of brain *circuits:* the coordinated interplay of several interconnected brain areas in creating specific mind states and behaviours. Human emotions, for example, involve several circuits and many interconnected areas.

In computer terms, we can look at the reptilian brain and the limbic system as largely "hardwired." The programs that control what these ancient brains do are embodied in the physical structure itself, in unchangeable *read-only memory* (ROM). The neocortex is different. Although it does have certain inherited, "wired-in" structures, neocortical memory is the changeable *random access* type (RAM). The neocortex can be programmed by that process we call learning.

With this sophisticated three-tiered brain working for the body/mind, why aren't our inner lives a piece of cake? Why don't we experience continuous joy? Our inner lives are not more blissful because key parts of that brain were designed and programmed by evolution to prod us toward survival and reproduction. Personal and species survival were the operating values embodied in the hard-wired programs of the ancient brains. Strong emotion arrived with the evolution of the limbic brain, and from then on fixed-pattern stereotyped behaviours were coloured with emotion. These new forms of pleasure and pain were potent mechanisms that helped to keep human beings and other mammals on the survival and reproduction track. Today, this ancient-brain programming frequently leads us to view present happenings from a reactive perspective. Human minds frequently fill with anger or fear or intense desire, and human actions often follow suit.

Much research has been done to establish the physical basis of the emotions and of emotion-backed behaviours, such as rage, aggression, flight, eating, and sex. Paul MacLean and many other researchers contributed to this effort, and an appreciable body of knowledge has accumulated.[5] As a result, the nature of the problem we humans face in reaching inner and outer peace has become clearer.

Let's look at outer peace first, and those overt behaviours that are anything but peaceful. What is it that prompts the heavy, reactive behaviours, and what can be done to avoid them?

Both nature and nurture, genes and environment, play their parts. Animal experiments have helped us to understand the genetically-determined side of the problem. One technique used extensively by experimenters was to probe and electrically stimulate the reptilian and limbic brains of several types of mammals. By moving the probe, electrically stimulating a new area, and watching the behaviour of the animal, they were able to map these structures. A second technique involved surgery. Sometimes researchers made lesions in various parts of the old brains; sometimes they removed parts of those brains surgically.

One important finding was that the structures, functions, and maps were similar in all the mammals tested – and in humans too, though much of the data on humans was arrived at less intrusively.[6] That part of the limbic system called the hypothalamus plays a major role in these basic behaviours. Cats, rats, and monkeys all had an area of the hypothalamus that, if stimulated, triggered aggressive behaviour. Stimulating nearby areas triggered sexual, flight, and eating behaviours in these animals.

In humans, oral and sexual gratification often go together; sex and aggression do too. The mapping technique revealed that the close connection between oral and sexual gratification is rooted in physical brain structure. The stimulation of certain areas of the limbic system will trigger simultaneous oral and sexual behaviour. The researchers found a similar situation with sex and aggression. Some monkeys get erections as part of their dominance behaviour toward other males. In humans, sex and aggression are found together in rape and sadistic sexual activity. And some hunters, I have been told, get an erection when they shoot an animal.

In many species of mammals the male is more aggressive, more of the time, than the female – and this is true of human beings. In Canada during a recent year, 86 per cent of the adults charged with homicide were men. Also, 98.5 per cent of the adults charged with aggravated sexual assault were men. As I understand it, extensive comparative research on male/female psychology has revealed only two clear differences between the sexes: males are more aggressive than females, and females are more nurturing than males.[7]

Why does this difference in aggression exist? Why are males more prone to violence? Research on rats has revealed a suspicious biological difference. It seems that the hypothalamus develops differently in males than it does in females. Melvin Konner reported on a study by G. Raisman and P. M. Field:

> In the most forward portion of the hypothalamus, the deepest nucleus of the brain, male and female rats differed in the density of synaptic connections among local neurons. Furthermore, castration of males just after birth would leave them with the female brain pattern, and injection of testosterone into females – likewise just after birth – would give them the male pattern.[8]

In mammals, the basic brain design is female. The male variation of that design develops if testosterone is present at certain critical times.

We can't draw extensive conclusions from this evidence, nor use it to deny the key role that culture plays when it approves of male aggression and violent behaviour in various circumstances. Still, it's clear that the urges themselves are biology based, and the limbic brain and its hypothalamus are potential troublemakers. Thus, I lose nothing by playing it safe and assuming that they're going to cause me, a male, even more trouble than they would a female. Konner said, ". . . we can have little doubt that we would all be safer if the world's weapon systems were controlled by average women instead of by average men."[9] It's hard to find fault with that statement. And if we want to move from average to wiser-than-average, then it seems clear that the men among us will need to work harder at the task than the women. For us men, average is farther from wisdom.

CHAPTER

3

Ignorance

Have you ever missed the chance to apply for a job because you didn't hear about the opening until it was too late? Have you ever run a stop sign because you were absorbed in thought and just didn't see it? Have you ever based your actions on what someone told you, only to discover that what you'd been told wasn't true? Data that is missing because we were never exposed to it, data that is missing because we failed to pay attention, and garbled or erroneous data can all cause problems in our lives. What we don't know *can* hurt us.

Back in Chapter 1, I mentioned the *system* perspective that helped me understand aspects of the physical world. In a similar way, the *analog* perspective helped me understand an important aspect of the mental world: the acquiring of information. I found in the writings of the General Semanticists and Julian Jaynes this most helpful way of looking at the relationship between physical reality and our mental experience of it. It is not the whole story. It deals only with our ordinary sense-based, information-based knowing. It doesn't deal with non-descriptive, intuitive kinds of knowing – knowing through identity. Still, since much of our knowledge is based on analogs of one sort or another, it is helpful in countless circumstances. If we understand how it works and become aware of its limitations we're less likely to be led astray.

Knowing by analogy works like this. Each small region of the cosmic process has its informational, space-based, time-based nature – its reality of form and function. We perceive that reality, and come to know something about its nature, through communications from it to our senses. Those communications are received by eyes, ears, nose, or other sensory apparatus, and translated by that apparatus into neuronal impulses. Then, from this neuronal information, the brain creates a subjective experience – a mental metaphor or analog that stands for, and represents in consciousness, the external reality.

These mental constructs may be just simple symbols or labels such as a specific taste or odour or colour. Or they may be complex analogs involving informational patterns in space or time – a complete scene, for example, or a melody. Consciousness analogs are mental maps that parallel the external reality to some limited extent. Perceptual experience is an analog of objective reality in the same sense that a map is an analog of a territory, or a photograph is an analog of a scene.

An analog is not usually constructed of the same material or "medium" as the reality from which it is derived. A physical map may be made of paper and show roads as red lines. The territory it describes is not made of paper and the roads are not red, but the map is still useful. It is organized or arranged in a way that shows a consistent similarity to the organization of the original. I eventually came to see that the essence of the parallelism is common *information*.

My head turns and my eyes focus. But what awareness sees is not the outer world at all. What it "sees" is part of this amazing informational show being created by the brain – the perception-connected part. Yes, this aspect of the show bears some relationship to what is going on outside the body, but the show itself – that world of colour and form and smell and touch and taste and sound – is 100 per cent brain-generated mind event. I find it easy to forget that colour doesn't exist "out there." Just light of different wavelengths. Sound doesn't exist out there. Just air waves of varying pressure and frequency. Odours don't exist out there. Just molecules drifting in the air. The whole of my subjective life really is an informational show created by the functioning of my brain. My usual assumption – that I'm in direct contact with what's going on in the outer world – is an illusion. I'm in contact all right, but it's a pretty distant, tenuous, and incomplete contact.

Recall your early childhood and imagine, if you can, your first encounter with an orange. The orange sits on the tray of your high chair, bathed in sunlight. Its surface reflects some of that light, particularly light having a wavelength of 0.6 microns. As you faced the orange some of the reflected light entered your eyes and – on each retina – formed an optical image of that orange. A stream of electro-chemical impulses then travelled from excited photoreceptors to your brain. There, somehow, the brain took into account the differences in colour sensitivity between the different types of photoreceptors, and noted which ones had been stimulated. It even took note of the blind spot in each eye where the optic nerve goes through the retina, and filled in the hole that would otherwise appear in the image.[10] The brain then generated a set of output impulses that somehow interfaced with awareness, and modulated it – producing the mental experience of seeing that orange. When you got older you hung verbal tags on such experiences. The labels for this one might have been *visual, round, orange-coloured, textured surface*.

Other parts of the brain also generate neuronal patterns, patterns representing other aspects of the reality we call an orange. In your first encounter with an orange you not only created a visual analog of it, but also an odour analog, a taste analog, and a touch analog. You experienced the fragrance analog of the essential-oil molecules given off by the peel. You experienced the sweet/sour taste analog of the sugar molecules and acid ions present inside the orange. And you experienced the touch-sensation analog of the juice dribbling down your hands. With all four of these very different analogs being generated by the same object, you perceived the reality of that orange just about as completely as one can with the unaided senses.

The awareness that observes these brain-generated analogs is organized spatially. It is really an x–y field of awareness affected by x–y fields of data, with a crude synthesized z dimension. (This z-axis or depth effect is apparently simulated by data-combining techniques not much different from those that produce holographic images.)[11]

You might want to stop for a moment and investigate this awareness field for yourself. If I look straight ahead, and move my hands around to find the edges of the visually-active part of the field, I conclude that it's about one unit high and three or four wide. If I then put a bottle of perfume under my nose, the experience of odour fills much of this same field – being most intense in the centre, less so at the edges. If next I bite into a piece of fruit and pay attention to my experience of taste as I chew it, I find that taste occupies a more sharply defined zone than odour. Taste sensations appear in a horizontally-oriented oval located below the centre of visual data. Touch, body sensations, and sounds also appear in the awareness field, sometimes extending beyond the edges of the visual data. The location of most body feelings and sensations is sharply defined, while the direction of most sounds is just roughly indicated.

All these spatially-organized layers of data are, like multiple transparent overlays, simultaneously projected onto awareness. This data modulates or "waves" awareness, impressing transient informational patterns upon it. Experience – mind content – consists of these awareness waves or modulations.

These different types of sensory data can appear superimposed on each other because the data that modulates awareness is brain output data, not perceptual input data. The different external stimuli received by eyes, ears, taste buds, etc. all produce similar nervous system impulses and electrochemical brain happenings. It is these physical brain happenings – not the original stimuli – that somehow modulate awareness and create subjective experience. Because our sensory apparatus converts the different types of input data into neuronal data, it's not too surprising that awareness can watch all inputs – separately or simultaneously – in one spatial array. What goes on in the brain appears analogous to what goes on in a TV studio's video switching and mixing board. There, the output of several cameras (and other video sources) can be combined in a controlled way into a single video output – the one the home viewer watches.[12]

In summary, subjective mind consists of a field of awareness populated by mental "objects," mind contents. These contents are a patterned disturbance or modulation of awareness – created, it seems clear, by the patterned firing of countless neurons and related chemical activity. Different kinds of information – bodily sensations, thoughts, images, sounds, and emotional moods and reactions – are presented to the subjective field via these electro-chemical energy transfers. We might say that the human and animal variety of mind exists where primal awareness has neuronal processes as its object. This mind is the fundamental reality accessible to a sentient being. Everything else we "know to be a fact" (such as the nature of the objective world out there) is really speculation based on inferences from the experienced patterns.

Language plays a special role in our acquisition of information, and understanding this role can help us avoid language-caused ignorance. It turns out that, just as perceptions and mental models are analogs of objective reality, our verbal statements are analogs of our subjective reality. Language is an analog created word by word and phrase by phrase from aspects of our conscious experience. Like other analogs, language is reversible; it can also be used to guide us in generating conscious experience. Language allows me, in some degree, to share the subjective experience of another person. The person speaking to me creates a verbal analog of his experience. In turn his words, his verbal analog, helps to create similar content within my mind – a more or less accurate replication, or at least understanding, of his state of mind.

We need to keep in mind that it's also possible to create verbal analogs of mind contents – subjective realities – that have *no* real-world analog. One thrill of my childhood was listening each Saturday morning to a radio programme called "Let's Pretend." Each week I would listen to the dramatization of a different fairy tale. The words from my radio created castles and witches and giants and princesses in my mind. Each programme ended with an invitation to write for tickets to see a broadcast if you were ever in New York. My chance eventually came. We sent for tickets, and I remember the excitement of walking into that theatre. It turned out to be one of the great disappointments and disillusionments of my life. There, on stage, were no castles, nor witches, nor giants – just ordinary people, wearing ordinary clothes, standing still, speaking into microphones.

This experience has been a reminder to me that language is strictly a link between one consciousness and another. It's a means by which one person can try to share his or her *subjective* reality with another person. "Let's Pretend" allowed me to experience the subjective reality of Hans Christian Andersen and the Brothers Grimm, that was all. Words emanate from someone's subjective experience, not from what is going on in the world.

Words can indirectly link us with objective reality, but only if three conditions are met. First, the speaker or writer's conscious experience must be an accurate analog of the objective reality. Second, the word-analog of that conscious experience must parallel the experience itself. Third, the person receiving the communication must have an appropriate vocabulary or mental library – not only of words, but also of concepts, prior experiences, and mind states that can be triggered by those words. (If I'd never seen pictures of castles and witches and giants the words would have meant nothing to me.)

We can begin to see how tenuous and iffy the process of understanding reality through words really is. "The map is not the territory," said Korzybski, the father of General Semantics. True. And understanding someone's verbal description is akin to making a map of a map of a map of the territory. (Objective reality is the territory. My conscious experience of it is map #1. My words about my experience of it are map #2. Your conscious experience constructed from my words is map #3.) The process obviously works well enough, accurately enough, for many purposes. We are involved with words much of the time. But the danger is clear. Something of the essence of the previous stage is lost each time we make a map of that stage and from that point on rely only on the map. As the General Semanticists point out, each analog is an abstract – a partial rendering of its source. An analog preserves and transmits only some aspects of the original. Something is always left out. We can never come to understand or know the form-and-function aspects of reality in an absolute, complete, or perfect sense.

Keeping in mind the tenuous, analogic nature of the process of understanding can help us avoid some information-gathering pitfalls. For one thing, the value of first-hand experience becomes evident. First-hand experience allows us to make first-hand maps – not this map of a map of a map stuff. If we are careful observers, these first-hand maps are likely to be more accurate. Also, we need first-hand experience if we want other people's words to make sense to us. Broad first-hand experience enriches that library of experiences and mind-states stored away in memory. It enriches the pool of material waiting to be pulled into awareness by the words of others. (Words that trigger nothing cannot further our understanding.)

The importance of attentiveness is also apparent. The words *ignorance* and *ignore* both come from the same Latin root. They are connected in everyday life too. What we ignore, what we don't pay attention to, never becomes part of our storehouse of data. Thus, inattention – ignore-ance – contributes to our ignorance.

C H A P T E R

4

Delusion

We are ignorant to the extent that we lack useful information. We are deluded to the extent that we think we understand but don't. Delusion can be a bigger problem than ignorance. In ignorance (when needed information is missing or garbled) we often know that a problem exists and take steps to acquire the missing data. In delusion (when we misinterpret valid data) we are often convinced that we have no problem at all – and thus are in deeper trouble.

In this chapter I invite you to consider the proposition I put forth earlier, that

1. the perspectives we use to interpret information are just as important as the information itself, and

2. the use of flawed or inappropriate perspectives can block the path to wisdom.

Delusion comes in various forms; let's look at three of the more serious troublemakers.

Bad Models

What do we really mean when we say that we *know* something? There is a growing consensus that *knowing* an informational reality means having some sort of mental construct stored away in memory that fits the data we have just received.

In the case of ordinary direct perception the implicit question seems to be, "Is the current perception familiar, or isn't it?" Have you ever noticed that infants at about nine months respond to their mothers' faces with a smile, and strange faces with fear? In a supermarket, do you tend to buy familiar items and pass up unfamiliar ones? Does an unfamiliar word stop the flow of your reading? We feel informed if we can match the current perception with past ones; we feel uninformed if we can't – and possibly fearful or curious.

Intellectual knowing is slightly different. We might think of it as *model-ordered* perception. Here the raw perceptual data is compared with the brain's file of abstract cognitive structures – theories, concepts, and other mental models. If what we perceive fits one of those abstract mental schemes, we get the feeling that we understand. If it doesn't fit any of them, we feel disquieted – and might try to create one that does fit. (We sometimes call this "looking for an explanation.")

There are countless examples of this model-oriented perception. A psychiatrist, in perceiving the words and behaviour of a patient, sometimes sees and hears those words in the context of a therapeutic theory. An electronic technician sees a faulty TV picture in the context of schematic diagrams and malfunctioning circuitry. And in this book, I the author lose you the reader every time I attempt to explain something using a concept, model, or metaphor that is unfamiliar to you.

Because awareness and direct perception are arranged spatially, it shouldn't be too surprising that much of our abstract thinking also involves spatial arrangements of data. Perhaps you picture the passage of time as a panorama of events with the past on the left and the future on the right – or the future ahead and the past behind. Creating a spatial analog of time is one way of conceiving of this aspect of reality.

To grasp mathematical concepts we often spatialize them. We picture piles of money, and bar graphs, and x–y co-ordinates, and curves. We spatialize the authority/responsibility situation in a corporation when we visualize it as an organization chart showing *lines* of communication and *chains* of command, as well as *positions* of relative power and status. Maslow arranged human needs in a hierarchy which is often visualized as a triangle with the *lower* physical and psychological needs at the base and the *higher* self-actualization needs at its peak. We use network diagrams to picture the flow of communication, and we again spatialize time when we generate those patterns of events called critical path scheduling charts.

There are also many concepts that do not involve spatial organization but which, like spatial concepts, are powerful tools for making sense of our experience. Several of these non-spatial concepts come to mind: Goal-seeking or *cybernetic* systems. *Feedback*, both positive and negative. The computer program and its role in guiding information-processing activities. And *information* itself. Countless others exist in fields like economics, political science, and psychology which could help us better understand what is going on. There is a price for making such concepts our own, of course: time and mental effort.

Until I began reading extensively back in the '60s, I had limited my own exploration of the conceptual world pretty much to technical concepts. This was unfortunate. From the day I was born I had been bombarded by the data of everyday life, yet I wasn't making the best possible sense of that data. Once begun, my reading allowed me to share the perspectives and mental models of people like Maslow, Sartre, and Kazantzakis. These writers introduced me to general patterns that helped me make sense of the hodge-podge of specifics I continually faced. Into their models I plugged the data of my own life, and tested it for accuracy of fit. Where a fit existed, I was likely to see that perspective, model, or metaphor as a useful explanatory tool.

The feeling that we understand is usually emotionally satisfying and calming to us. Sometimes, though, we forget that the subjective feeling of understanding is not necessarily the same as truly understanding. Countless millions of people, for example, used the story of creation in Genesis as their mental model of the origin of life and human beings. They took it to be a literal description of the way things happened, and derived from it the warm reassuring feeling that they understood. It now appears that the story – taken literally – is not an accurate account of what happened. Although people felt that they understood, they did not.

Isaac Newton came up with some beautifully simple equations to describe the motion of physical bodies. These equations, these models, gave Newton and his contemporaries this feeling of understanding to a high degree. It was not until Einstein arrived at a new set of equations which included relativistic effects that it became clear that Newton's model was not perfectly accurate. Einstein's model paralleled what was really going on in the universe more closely than Newton's.

No, the feeling that we understand is not enough. All sorts of bad models can give us that feeling. Analogs are rarely, if ever, perfect. Something is almost always lost in the translation from one medium to another. And a model is always an abstract. We can never come to understand or know the form-and-function aspects of reality in an absolute, complete, or perfect sense. What we do know we know second-hand through our analogs, through our models. We're stuck with models. But some models are less defective than others. We don't have to be stuck with bad ones. And **it is by finding, creating, and using models which prove to be adequate, close-fitting analogs of reality that we come to understand what is going on in an objective sense – and not just think that we understand it.**

It's often the case that a model parallels part of reality well and the rest poorly or not at all. Also, a model may parallel reality under a certain range of conditions but not under all conditions. Our mental spatialization of quantity, for example, works for small and medium amounts, but fails us when we try to grasp the very large (millions and billions) or the very small (millionths and billionths). Because the limitations of models are not always taken into account, models are sometimes inappropriately applied. A close fit in one situation may lead us to conclude that "this is a good model," and we mistakenly apply it in a situation where the fit is not good. Maslow's picture of self-actualization, for instance, came out of experience with people in a Western industrial culture. He realized, near the end of his life, that in a culture like Mexico, self-actualization would probably involve less autonomy and need for privacy, and more commitment to family, friends, and community. Since it is rare for a model's range-of-fit to be specified, this kind of problem may be harder to discover than a total conflict with reality.

One way of dealing with this type of situation is to modify the model – perhaps by adding conditions or caveats. Another is to use multiple models. There is no single model, for example, that fully parallels the nature of light. We can, however, get along satisfactorily by using two partial and incomplete models. Back in my design engineering days, whenever I worked with lenses and diffraction gratings I used the wave model of light. When I worked with low-light-level photocells I used the particle model. Using two models was my pragmatic solution. Clinical psychologists use multiple models all the time. There are dozens of models of mind processes, and a pragmatic therapist will use the one that best fits the patient's situation.

When you think about it, because any model covers only certain aspects of a given reality you'd expect multiple models to be the rule rather than the exception. One of this book's strong messages is that **most situations deserve to be viewed from many perspectives. Any one perspective on a situation, even if it is a totally valid perspective, reveals just a tiny bit of the truth of that situation. Additional valid perspectives reveal more.**

A related problem arises when we meet one-of-a-kind realities – realities that have no consciousness analogs at all. Such things exist. They are aspects of the process that have no parallel in human experience. For these realities we have no raw material, no appropriate snatches of mind content to pull from memory and use in building a mental model. It's unfortunate, but among these "strange" realities are some of the most basic, most fundamental aspects of our existence. Take the four-dimensional space-time of Minkowski and Einstein, for example. My brain can create three-dimensional analogs, but not four-dimensional ones. Or take light again. My brain can generate wave-like analogs, and it can generate particle-like analogs. But it boggles when it tries to combine the two into one. And there are realities that are completely informationless such as pure awareness, the ground of mind. Is it any wonder that the ancient seers were reduced to using terms like Void, Nirvana, and Tao in discussing root realities? When dealing with formless realities we can only *point at* them with words. We can only *refer to* their existence. They are inherently indescribable.

Seeing separation rather than unity

Back in Chapter 1, I referred to the ability to see the underlying unity as a characteristic of wisdom. Here I'm saying that our failure to see that unity results from a delusion – albeit, an almost universal one. Albert Einstein had this to say:

> A human being is a part of the whole called by us universe, a part limited in time and space. He experiences himself, his thoughts and feelings as something separated from the rest, a kind of optical delusion of his consciousness. This delusion is a kind of prison for us, restricting us to our personal desires and to affection for a few persons nearest to us.[13]

Most of us have spent our entire lives thinking of the universe as outer environment. We've always considered persons to be separate and distinct beings or objects. I look at you, and you look at me and yes, our sense of sight confirms it – we are separate beings. Or are we?

The evolutionary view of what is going on in the universe bases its case for unity on the unity of physical process. In this view the universal process is the one basic entity. We humans are simply localized nodes of process – nodes that happen to be aware.

There is, of course, just one real situation involving the nature and relationship of person and universe. But there are various ways of viewing that situation, various mental models of it. Here we are concerned with two of these models. I'll call our normal way of looking at things the *object* model. It's the one that Einstein called a delusion. Most of us are prisoners of that model. To free ourselves we don't need to abandon that model completely. But we do need to be able to switch to the second model, the *unitive* model, in circumstances where it is more appropriate.

When we view the situation from our usual sense-oriented perspective we see this familiar object model. We tend to ignore our links with the rest of the universe because they don't generate loud sensory messages. We find it natural to view human beings as isolated independent entities. But when we stand back and consider our human situation in context, consider it from the perspective of the universe-as-a-whole, we see a very different picture. We see atoms from the primordial explosion, and additional atoms constructed inside the stars of universe, making their way to the newly-forming earth. We then see a lengthy evolutionary process. During that process the means develop to direct roughly 10,000,000,000,000,000,000,000,000,000 (10^{28}) of these primordial and star-forged atoms at a time into temporary, mobile, intelligent, human-shaped pieces of universe. We might call this the *structural connection*.

These intelligent chunks of universe are also tied to the process in other ways. The *energy connection* provides them with the continuous supplies of energy they need to think and to do. Solar energy is intercepted by green growing things that convert it into chemical energy. These plants, directly or indirectly, supply each human subsystem with stored solar energy. They also supply other chemicals needed for building and repairs.

Because some materials taken in are not used, and because internal processes generate unwanted chemicals, each subsystem also has its *waste connection* with the larger process.

These universe subsystems need continuous supplies of oxygen, and they generate quantities of CO_2. The atmosphere of earth provides this *gas connection* almost everywhere, continuously.

The wider universe is also linked to its human localizations with an *information connection*. The senses provide one-way information flow to the subsystem from the larger system (including its other subsystems). The *action connection* involves a flow in the opposite direction, from subsystem to system-at-large. This reverse flow includes not only coded communications, but all other forms of doing as well.

No, people aren't the independent entities they think they are. Each of us has six real, absolutely necessary links connecting us with the rest of the universe – structural, energy, waste, gas, information, and action connections. Human beings are *open systems*, which is another way of saying that we are not independent, but are parts of a larger system.

Fortunately for personal mobility, these subsystem links have been provided without the need for physical cables and hoses. Because of that, they are like the other subtle, silent realities around us: they are all too easy to ignore. Yet these connections with the larger universe are just as real as if they had been made with six-foot-long pieces of wire and tubing. We humans are, in a concrete and non-mystical sense, intelligent nodes of the larger universe.

There is an analogy that might prove helpful. The relationship of the universe to its people outcrops is similar to that of ocean to its wave outcrops. We watch an individual wave rise up from the continuum, from the background of ocean. It rises to a white-capped peak which bubbles, churns, and froths. For a moment there is intense localized activity. This spot in the ocean has its own active uniqueness. Countless independent lines of cause and effect have intersected here to create for a brief moment a unique one-time occurrence – a localized intensification in the overall process of ocean. In another moment the frothing and bubbling subsides, the peak recedes, and the uniqueness diffuses back into the background of ocean process from which it arose a moment before. Soon, its atoms will have spread and become part of other ripples and swells and whitecaps. In the same sense that a wave is ocean, a person is universe.

Alan Watts used another analogy. He said, "We do not 'come into' this world; we come *out* of it, as leaves from a tree." The universe configures itself into nodes of awareness and action much as a tree configures itself into buds and leaves. A tree's individual leaves come in the spring and drop off in the fall. We have no trouble identifying the tree as the organism, with buds and leaves as parts of that organism. So it is with human beings. Persons are buds of universe that stay for a season. Then – after having made their contribution to the whole – they, like the leaves, disintegrate.

It didn't take me long to feel intellectually comfortable with this second model of person-universe – this unitive model. The challenge, of course, is to feel it so deeply in the guts that we live our lives by it. The object model is our easy-to-see built-in model because it helped our ancestors to survive. But times have changed. We find ourselves, today, with those tremendous technology-based powers capable of destroying as well as building. For us it is the unitive view that has survival value. Gregory Bateson once admitted that he found it difficult to think in this unitive way. But at the same time he said that we shouldn't trust the policy decisions of people who are not able to.

Misidentification

The main thing blocking the unitive view, in the assessment of several spiritual traditions, is inappropriate identification. Particularly troublesome is identification with the body and with mind contents. The Buddha called this identification *wrong view of self.* I call it the *identity delusion.* The problem is this: Associated with awareness is a primal sense of identity, a sense of existing, an I AM sense. Evolution led humans (and other beings) to associate this sense of identity not with awareness itself, but with the objects of awareness – most often, with the body and with mind contents. Later, human cultures encouraged other identifications – identifications with ethnic origin, social role, organization, nation, etc.

Any identification lends power to the object of identification. The extra survival power that accompanied identification with the local body/mind was useful tens of thousands of years ago when conditions of life were more marginal than they are in the industrial nations today. It had survival value for the individual in those times, and thus for the species. When you feel that you are the local body/mind, and *only* the body/mind, you tend to devote large amounts of energy and attention to enhancing and preserving the personal self. This improves the chances of survival for that particular body/mind – and thus the chances of its genes being passed on. This was great for the species, but unpleasant for the poor individual who paid the price in fear, anger, lust, jealousy, and other forms of emotional pain.

Awareness is primary reality, but our minds have never realized that. Instead of identifying with the underlying ground of mind, the primal sense of identity usually becomes attached to mind *contents.* We get lost in that show called daily living, or an engrossing movie, or those shows called dreams that awareness watches while the body sleeps. We project the sense of reality that belongs with awareness onto something else – onto whatever awareness is aware of. Are patterns of light on a movie screen *me?* No, but I've been fooled into thinking so many times, as my heart rate escalated and the adrenalin pumped. A movie is information on a physical screen, translated into informational patterns of firing neurons which then modulate awareness. The experience of everyday life is similar: information from external and internal sources, translated into patterns of firing neurons, is experienced by awareness. Does it make sense to identify with any of this? Yet we always have.

The ordinary everyday "I" is a phantom created by the processes of perceiving, reacting emotionally, and thinking. Our brain creates the ego, the "I," the *voice of the system*, to represent the local process in its dealings with the external world. This "I" has many aspects. It is the rationalizing verbosity of the left brain hemisphere. It is reactivity in all its forms. It is the mind's resistance to whatever is happening in the present moment. All the elements that together make up the illusion of a separate self – the identification-tinged reactions, emotions, and judgements – are simply informational events within the subjective field. It is the subjective field itself, not its contents, that is the natural home of that sense-of-self identity. We have been confused about what is subject, what is object, and what is *me*.

Giving up this local-process identification is difficult for several reasons. One is perceptual. We see ourselves as separate beings. We don't see all those absolutely necessary connections with the larger process. Another is the strength of the ego, the strength of the self concept. We find it difficult to become as little children. The ego does not want to die. The ego is attached to *its* accomplishments. It doesn't like to see the causal links between those accomplishments and outside influences that it cannot take credit for – good genes, good environment, information picked up from elsewhere, opportunities set up by external forces, etc. It won't admit that everything that happens is, in fact, the universe's accomplishment – the accomplishment of the Self-at-large if you will.

The spiritual teachers of old were making perfect sense when they told us to abandon our egos and devote ourselves to the great ONE. Their message in today's words might be: "Face facts. See what is. Identifying with the subsystem is a meaningless dead end. To be significant you must go beyond your preoccupation with the body/mind subsystem and act in the service of the larger process." A leaf preoccupied with its own leafness – and neglectful of its function as tree – would not be actualizing its potential as a leaf-shaped subsystem of tree. Human beings preoccupied with their own illusion of separateness and individuality – and neglectful of their function as universe – are not actualizing their potential as human-shaped subsystems of universe.

The identity delusion not only causes external problems, it also damages us psychologically; it causes needless suffering. Each infant and young child undergoes the experience of individuation. According to the psychologists who study these things, we start life with no sense of separateness, and during our first few years gradually arrive at the consensus view of identity which then remains with us.

We are not totally happy with this new view, however, and throughout our lives there are times when we unconsciously try to go back, when we do things in an attempt to regain that feeling of connectedness that we lost. We use various names for the place that we seek: Happiness. Home. Belonging. Relationship. Community. But they are all substitutes and aliases. What we seek at the deepest level is our lost sense of oneness, our lost sense of identity with everything.

The finding lies in abandoning all the external searches, and recognizing that the psychological experience of individuation that we underwent – while a necessity for conducting everyday life – led us into a delusion. The finding lies not in regression, in some attempt to create a substitute womb. It lies in transcendence: in recognizing the delusion for what it is. It lies in seeing clearly for the first time the identity that has always existed. It lies in making a gestalt flip to that other perspective on our situation, to that other way of seeing and interpreting the data of life and existence. Our most fundamental or "true" identity resides in the permanent medium of existence, not in any of the temporary informational modulations that overlay that medium. We are Awareness-Energy, the eternal ground of subjective and objective being.

The Garden of Eden story can be interpreted in light of the delusion. When, as small children, we began to acquire knowledge, we lost our prior sense of oneness. During our first few years of life we encountered the tree of knowledge. We became immersed in, and eventually adopted, the whole informational world of distinction and difference. The apple is the mythical symbol for that informational world, and the normal child ends up grasping it, ends up making a not totally happy choice for separate existence.

We adults can't undo the lives we've lived to date – and that isn't the answer, even if we could. Much of the knowledge we acquire about the informational world while under the delusion's spell is appropriate and useful. There are indications, too, that it may not be possible to make it through the first four levels in Maslow's hierarchy of needs – the physiological, security, belongingness, and esteem need levels – without a strong ego-identification. We may need to build an ego before we can destroy it.[14] But we can look back at what has happened. We can see that the individuation process (that metaphorical eating of the fruit) did delude us into abandoning our prior sense of oneness. And we can entertain the possibility that the sense of oneness still lies within us, just waiting to be recognized.

Each of us knows what it's like to feel happy, to feel at home, to feel a sense of belongingness. We just need to claim those feelings as legitimately ours. Here. Now. In the past we have looked at happiness, feeling at home, and belongingness as goals to be attained through externals – through a search for pleasure, possessions, the perfect house, the right community, the perfect relationship. As long as we continue to connect those mental states with external searching and finding, we'll never more than briefly glimpse them. If, however, we recognize happiness, feeling at home, and belongingness as characteristics of a subjective sense of oneness, then we can drop the external chase and reclaim our intrinsic connectedness right here, right now.

In reality, the delusion did not destroy the pre-existing oneness. The primal unity was never broken; an *illusion* of separateness arose. Therefore, there is no need to mount a search for the primal oneness. We simply need to recognize it, to *re-cognize* it. In coming chapters, we'll look at what is involved in doing this.

Earlier I noted that cultures, too, induce people to make misidentifications. In the recruit who enlists, goes through military training, and then to war, the subjective "I" may become identified more strongly with the nation (or the nation's ideology) than with body and mind contents. Identification with the body may even be abandoned completely, causing this soldier to willingly "give his life for his country." In some cultures, an intense ethnic or religious identity is similarly encouraged and developed.

Cultural influences sometimes induce the subjective "I" to identify strongly with a life role or some slot in the societal or organizational structure. If we ask a person who they are, we often get a role-identified response, don't we? "I am . . . a teacher . . . the president . . . a housewife." Similarly, in people who are intensely involved with one aspect of life for a prolonged period the subjective "I" may identify with that aspect. Out of such situations can emerge strong identifications with a particular gender, sexual orientation, subculture, or institution.

A case can be made that this mechanism of arbitrary identification now threatens the whole species. Arthur Koestler, Eric Fromm, and other researchers into the causes of war, have fingered the identification phenomenon as a fundamental troublemaker.[15] Identification with nation or race results in a we/they in-group/out-group division, often having deadly ramifications. Some level of respect for one's nation and ethnic ancestry is fine, but national governments frequently go to great lengths to make these identifications intense and binding. The means employed include reinforcements such as pledges of allegiance, rituals involving flags and royalty, reverence for national heroes, a too-positive portrayal of the nation in the news media, and blatant lies about the out-group. There is also likely to be punishment – even torture and death in some countries – for those who fail to identify with the nation and its aspirations.

Every strong identification other than identification with ALL or the underlying ONE has the potential to cause trouble, to downlevel the process. Here I include identification with person, nation, race, gender, community, and organization. All of these lesser identifications create an in-group and an out-group, a we and a they, an us and a them, a me and a you. Inherent in these lesser identifications are seeds of divisiveness and local advantage. Inherent in identification with Being, with ALL, with the ONE, are seeds of general well-being and overall upleveling.

CHAPTER

5

The Need for Wisdom

I have called the fundamental reality *Energy-Awareness,* but Being is more than just its active and receptive aspects. Were it not so cumbersome, I might have called the fundamental reality *Energy-Awareness-Guidance,* or *Energy-Awareness-Intelligence.* Intimately associated with energy and awareness is *intrinsic knowledge* that makes a guiding contribution to every event in the universe and the whole evolutionary process. This built-in intelligence consists of all the laws of nature, the values of all the universal constants, and possibly more.[16] In evolution, chance plays its part by setting up novel informational situations. Chance helps determine which *specific* potentials will be actualized. But it is this built-in guiding intelligence – this array of procedures, this matrix of recursive algorithms – that has established the potential for all happenings, and guides their unfolding.

The universe is clearly an information processor, though very different from computers of human design. The typical desktop computer runs one program at a time in serial fashion. You put information in. The information gets manipulated or "processed" in accord with the program's algorithm, its intrinsic plan. And the computer sends the changed information out.

In the information-processing cosmos, each physical situation, regardless of location, is input information. And each law of nature is a program, a functioning algorithm. But unlike the desktop computer that processes its data in serial fashion, the programs that guide the universe all function at the same time, in parallel. These laws-of-nature algorithms operate everywhere, simultaneously, continuously. It is parallel data processing in the extreme.

Because of this ongoing activity, the informational pattern of the universe constantly changes. An informational situation inherited from the previous instant gets turned into a new informational situation by the operation of various laws of nature. The process never rests. In the next instant the *new* pattern is subjected once again to that whole matrix of algorithms – and to the extent that the algorithms dictate, again, the pattern changes.

For the past 15 billion years or so, the algorithms that underlie and define the laws of nature have been applied again and again and again to every informational situation, everywhere in the universe. It's still happening. And it's called evolution.

I ask you to consider the possibility that the present era marks the beginning of a new phase in the evolutionary process. Evolution's first phase was characterized by the chance-and-necessity variety of evolution just described. Evolution did its thing, blindly but effectively creating and optimizing. Phase 1 evolution was extremely slow, but effective if you had the time to wait. In particular, Phase 1 techniques enabled the human body to evolve – with its sophisticated brain, its mobility, and its marvellous hands that can manipulate materials.

The question I put to you is this: Haven't these advanced capabilities, themselves, now become agents of evolution? For better or worse, haven't human capabilities moved evolution (here on earth at least) into an entirely new phase? Evolution in this second phase is mind-directed evolution. With the arrival of Phase 2, evolution no longer gropes forward blindly and automatically; human eyes and the human brain have given the process perceptual and conceptual sight. With its great power and speed, Phase 2 evolution now overrides the creeping-along Phase 1 process. Phase 1 evolution continues. But in those parts of the universe – such as earth – where Phase 2 capabilities exist, it must take a back seat as a cause of change.

Some years ago we humans started to practise this new style of evolution. We've already seen how rapidly things can be changed compared with the old way, and we've begun to see the dangers too. **The root problem is that Phase 2 projects are being directed by Phase 1 minds.** The harnessing of nuclear fission is one example. The negative impact of our high-tech lifestyle on the environment is another. And today we are going full speed ahead in the field of genetic engineering. I suspect that there is nothing *intrinsically* wrong with nuclear energy, technology-augmented comfort, and genetic engineering – nothing wrong **if pursued by wise people, acting with utmost caution, in accord with the highest aims and values.** But that is not the way it has been happening.

With Phase 1 minds and values guiding the process, the risks are great. In the view of many people today, unless this changes, unless the minds doing the directing are themselves guided by wisdom's values, Phase 2 on this planet is sure to be short-lived – and a disastrous failure.

Sophisticated brains, mobility, and the ability to manipulate materials were necessary before Phase 2 could begin, but they weren't all that was needed. Phase 2 also requires material sufficiency – a standard of living that gives large numbers of people the time, energy, and support systems needed for creativity. (Hungry people – grubbing for survival – are not likely to design silicon chips, conduct experiments in genetic engineering, or create great art.)

We humans are equipped with a wide array of mental potentials. The potentials evoked in the past under conditions of material scarcity (greed, hate, anger, etc.) helped the species survive. They prodded human beings to move toward material sufficiency. Now, with a basic level of material support in place in many parts of the world, those values and mind states hinder rather than help. Having served a useful purpose in Phase 1, they have become counterproductive in Phase 2.

Noisy, reactive, pain-filled Phase 1 minds are still the human norm. Despite this, whole societies of humans are attempting to get on with Phase 2 activities. It won't work. To help us appreciate this, I'd like to relate our data to a metaphor: the universe as a work of art – a work created by the universal process and its subsystems, and appreciated in the minds of those subsystems.

Before Roger Sperry did his split brain studies it was commonly felt that there were two types of people: logical, rational, practical people; and sensitive, creative, but impractical people. The tacit assumption was that logic and rationality were in conflict with openness, sensitivity, and creativity. You faced a trade-off: if you developed one set of qualities you would necessarily lose the other.

Then along came left-brain/right-brain theory that associated each of these sets of qualities with its own hemisphere of the brain's neocortex – and the assumptions changed. If rational thought and logic originated primarily in the left hemisphere, and creativity and artistic sensitivity originated primarily in the right, then there was no conflict – and no need for a trade-off.

What a freeing idea! Just because we had, in the past, developed one side of ourselves – one set of qualities, one brain hemisphere – didn't mean that we could not now develop the other. In fact, when you looked back at history and thought about people like Leonardo da Vinci, it was obvious that there had always been at least a few people who had developed both – and who deserved to be called complete, fully-developed human beings.

With that prologue in mind, let's now move to the metaphor itself. First, what is the purpose of art? The purpose, as I understand it, is to cause – through the generation of physical *works* – a qualitative change in the perceiver's conscious experience. My impression is that all good art uplevels our experience in some way. Either it produces uplifting feelings, or it helps us to know something or see something more clearly. Enhanced subjective experience is the goal of the art process.

The work that triggers the intellectual/emotional experience is an expression in some physical medium. It might be a medium with a memory like paint and canvas, or paper and ink, or film. Or it might be an ephemeral medium like a stage and moving players, or waves of air pressure coming from musical instruments.

An enhanced inner experience is the desired result. The work is the physical means by which that state is brought about. And of course it is the artist who creates the work. To create the work the artist employs two general aptitudes or skills. I will call them *holistic seeing* (right hemisphere stuff, according to many people), and *technical ability* (which they associate with the left). In *The Transformative Vision,* Jose Arguelles called them psychic impulse, and technique.

Each artist possesses these aptitudes to differing degrees. Some artists have little technical skill. They rely a lot on trial and error, randomness. An extreme case I once heard about was the prize-winning painting done by a chimpanzee. I assume that the chimp had little control over his doing, and very little ability to see holistically. But I also assume that the chimp produced many paintings. And I assume that someone who *could* see sorted through them and picked out the one that had a prize-winning arrangement of brush strokes. There are artists who have a good eye, and succeed because they throw a lot of stuff away.

There are also artists with considerable technical ability but no well-developed ability to see holistically. They often create pleasing works, but they don't create profound works. We admire their skill, but their works don't move us.

The great artists have two highly-developed cerebral hemispheres.

Keeping this limited overview of art in mind, let's consider the cosmic situation in which we find ourselves. The metaphoric parallels seem to be there. Minds capable of appreciating do exist: your mind, and mine, and minds at all levels in the hierarchy of earthly life. A work exists: the universe, and of particular interest to you and me, this local portion of it – our planet. Also, a process capable of producing, developing and refining that work exists: the evolutionary process including its latest local agents – "artists" like you and me. Let's see where the metaphor takes us.

Although the universe's reason for existing may not be the creation of uplifted states of mind, that notion doesn't seem totally far-fetched. Mental upleveling is, and has been, the focus of much activity. An observable trend of evolution is the development of increasingly sophisticated minds, minds capable of increasingly rich mental experience. Then, too, when I think about what we humans have been doing in our bumbling, inept, quasi-random way throughout history, I say to myself, "Hey! All along we've been trying to enhance subjective experience."

You and I spend much time doing things. We modify the physical world around us in countless ways. And although we may not think about it, doesn't most (if not all) of that doing have the same aim as art: to affect our state of mind? Don't we grow food, smoke cigarettes, build bridges, commit crimes, paint pictures, and save whales all in the service of someone's subjective experience – usually our own? True, most of us now and then sacrifice our personal enjoyment for periods of time. But when we make such a sacrifice isn't it in the hope of enhancing our own enjoyment later, or the hope of enhancing the enjoyment of another being? It seems that everything I've done today, from going to the toilet when I first got up this morning to writing this sentence was dedicated to enhancing someone's subjective experience. In this sense we do treat the world around us as an artist treats a work of art. That is, we do things in it and to it in hopes that the changed physical situation will enhance mental experience.

Was there a "psychic impulse" or holistic vision behind the universe? I see the evolutionary trends toward intelligence and other forms of sophisticated function as evidence of a loose, unfocused vision built right into the cosmic process, into the matrix of recursive algorithms that guide it. It strikes me as a gradually refining vision, one that takes specific form as time goes on, as entities evolve, and as those algorithms operate on more complex informational situations.

Technique, too, appeared primitive in the beginning. The early process comes across as a rather unskilled artist. We know, however, that although the process is slow, and fraught with failed experiments, it has produced amazing results. Recently, its capabilities got a large potential boost when it sprouted artist-agents in human form. The big pluses that we humans bring to the process are greatly increased speed, and the ability to work in media other than the carbon-based chemistry of life – media such as silicon-based microelectronics, for example.

For a long time, most human energy was needed just to survive. Then, between two and a half and three thousand years ago, groups of people in both the West and the East focused on self-development. Those in the Western World set about developing their rational side. They developed techniques, and analytical, rational thought processes. They concentrated on developing the ability to do. At the same time, those in the East set about developing their intuitive side. They worked out procedures for seeing and understanding in more holistic, intuitive ways. They concentrated on developing the ability to see.

We know what happened in the West. We know the tale of our industrialization and overindustrialization. Our development and overdevelopment. Our utilization of resources and overutilization of resources. With the best intention of improving our work of art, the results have been – charitably speaking – mixed. A chemical plant may enhance the subjective experience of the stockholders at dividend time, and perhaps my subjective experience if those chemicals make soles for my shoes. But it also may do great harm to the subjective experience of the thousands of people who live near, or down river from it.

What went wrong? Our metaphor is telling us that we've been messing around with a promising and already beautiful work of art – an emerging masterpiece – without bothering to become authentic artists first. We got good at technique, but we're still not worth a damn at holistic seeing. We've done many things well, but too often the wrong things.

Our metaphor points to the obvious: To avoid messing up our global work of art any further we need to become competent artists. We're only half artists now. To become whole we need to develop that other side of ourselves, and for most of the "doers" in Western society, the technically skilled ones, the decision makers, that "other" side is the intuitive, holistic-seeing side. We can start by looking to the experts and borrowing their techniques. From the East we can learn meditation and other spiritual practices. From the West we can learn how our most creative people go about seeing. We can learn the value of solitude and quiet-mindedness – staple techniques of artists – and try to incorporate them into our lives. We can also make a conscious attempt to free ourselves from psychological hangups and cultural biases that distort our perceptions. Most of us are already fairly knowledgeable. Isn't our next task to become wise?

As we've seen, our perceptions and memories are dealt with at various times by three key types of brain process: ancient-brain, intellect, and intuition. Each of these processes is capable of directing the human system and determining what a person does. Ancient-brain programming was appropriate for controlling behaviour in pre-civilized marginal circumstances, but it's not appropriate for more civilized sorts of living.

When we (as children and societies) became "civilized," cultural values took control. In our industrial cultures rationality became the primary mode of mental functioning – rationality in the service of the culture's dominant values. These values included material production and consumption, the acquisition of factual knowledge, participation in culture's projects and institutions, and pursuing the fruits of narcissistic individualism such as wealth, power, status, fame, etc.

Now, again, it's time for a transition. Intuitive, wisdom-based guidance is the appropriate mode for the post-industrial, millenial era, for the mind-directed phase of the evolutionary process. The possibility exists for each of us to become an artist-in-life, a wise person, a complete human being. Once we have done this, we – as person-shaped outcrops of universal process – can take full advantage of our short opportunity to add something to the universal work of art. We can enhance it for ourselves, for the other sensitive nodes of process who currently share the planet with us, and for those who come after.

It really is possible to go through all three of these stages in a lifetime. When we were two years old our ancient brains were in control much of the time. Parents and school pushed us (often unwillingly) through our first transition into the more civilized, more rational world of late childhood and adulthood. The second transition, from cultural control to wisdom control, can't be pushed. It is strictly voluntary, and at times arduous. The impediments to wisdom are real, but not insurmountable. The remaining chapters of this book are devoted to helping us get past them.

I would like to become one of the change agents of this new era – a fully-prepared, highly-effective Phase 2 evolutionary – one of those special people who have managed to become wise and free as well as knowledgeable. What, specifically, am I shooting for? What kind of person is it that I would like to be? The description that follows is my current image of these all-too-rare people. This is how I view their mind-sets and modes of functioning, their approach to problem solving and social transformation:

They have a wide, value-centred view of the problem. So often, readily available solutions to problems are not discovered because the problem itself has been defined too narrowly. The people I'm talking about, the wise and effective ones, start with the widest possible goal: they want to see the entire world process upleveled. There is some specific situation calling for action, but they see that situation in context – in the broadest possible context. They see the problematique – the larger problem matrix of which the present problem is just a part. They intentionally look from many angles and many perspectives. They are intensely interested in how the situation came to be and what maintains it. They gather as much data as possible but hold that data tentatively – remaining open to new data and fresh perspectives.

They have an extraordinary openness to possible solutions. The essence or core may not be negotiable – the value-centred part – but everything else is. And there are no unnecessary side issues complicating things. No committed-to ideology to maintain. No prior analysis that is sacrosanct. No fixed mindset or point of view. No divisions where there needn't be any. And no opponent. Ignorance, delusion, reactivity, and bad programming are the only opponents. There is no us against them, just a situation that must be enhanced and upleveled. This means there is no need for retribution, and no difficulty allowing those who have entrenched positions to save face, if that is possible.

They have an intense desire to find a solution. These people do not commit themselves lightly to a cause. They realize the preciousness of the body/mind's brief moment as a player in the game of existence. They are playing in earnest, and want their moment to count for as much as possible.

They have little personal vulnerability. Because, in their view, what the brain puts out is just stuff – to ignore or act upon as the wisdom dictates – it is difficult to push their buttons. Since even the death of the body is not viewed as the ultimate calamity, they are not easily controlled. They have learned how to maintain equilibrium and detachment, even in the midst of turmoil and threat.

They rely on the intuitive process for solutions. In wise and liberated people it is the intuitive process that comes up with those hard-to-find answers, and plays a major role in their decision making. Intuition can do so because:

1. The reactive and intellectual processes no longer dominate awareness and call the shots. (The minds of these people are relatively quiet and uncluttered.)

2. These people have spent years actively and open-mindedly searching for understanding. In the process, they have loaded their subconscious minds with much information about what *is*. Their intuitive processes, therefore, have a lot of valid data to draw on and integrate.

Having mastered the art of maintaining a quiet mind, they listen for communications from the Wisdom. Their intellectual models of reality are lightly held and subject to change, so they are open to intuitions that overturn present assumptions. They don't rush things. They are confident that if they co-operate with the process by keeping the mind quiet, and by feeding it with all available data, an optimum answer will come.

They continuously love and forgive. These people live compassionately. They see those they deal with as suffering beings – victims of inappropriate conditioning or programming by genes, culture, and life circumstances. When they look at someone, they see Being and its high values clothed in informational garments that don't fit, garments that obscure and distort the innate potential. What others call evil they see as unskilfulness and misdirection – the product of informational and algorithmic errors.

Many of today's issues aren't simple. To try to simplify them, to pull them out of their complex context and consider them in isolation, won't result in adequate solutions. There is hope that someday computer modelling will come of age and be a significant help in problem analysis and problem-solving. But the best problem-solving system around today is a person who is intelligent and wise, informed, open, and attentive. One who has looked widely, has seen, and has fed the intuitive process with all that it needs to weigh, balance, sift, sort, and come up with a tentative answer. The sort of person just described.

As I consider the characteristics of these people and the global situation an ethical imperative arises: **Become wise.** Become wise despite the lack of support from our present culture. Become wise despite all the impediments and seductions that inevitably get in the way. For doesn't everything that's worthwhile follow naturally and organically from wisdom? If we are wise, then ethical dilemmas vanish: we simply do what needs to be done. If we are wise, then we're ready for Phase 2.

CHAPTER

6

Dealing with Reactivity

The control of reactivity – reactive emotion and reactive behaviour – is both a cultural matter and a personal matter. Totally unbridled reactive behaviour is intolerable in any culture, yet channeled reactivity is often considered a cultural good. In our North American cultures, for example, a multi-billion-dollar advertising industry effectively keeps up our level of reactive desire. "Possess! Consume! Enjoy!" it exclaims. "Live the good life in all its dimensions!" Violence, when channeled against a culture's enemy, is another frequently encountered "cultural good."

Our culture, early in our lives, imposed upon us limits to reactive behaviour. It taught us how to behave. We learned what the culturally acceptable limits were. This learning took place in our neocortex, the largest, newest part of our brain. This part of the brain comes with (or develops as it matures) several facilitative structures into which culture-based learning imbeds itself. These structures define our intellectual potentials and include:

1. The linguistic deep structures that Noam Chomsky has written about – the built-in universal grammar that allows small children to quickly master whatever human language they are exposed to.

2. Ordinary musical, artistic, and mathematical sensibilities – and in rarer cases, giftedness in these areas.

3. Structures that allow us to analyze – to perform analytical, linear, rational data processing.

4. Structures that allow us to synthesize – to perform creative, holistic, intuitive data processing.

5. Gear-shifting structures that move us toward higher levels of psychological growth when circumstances are favorable: Maslow's "hierarchy of needs," and Joseph Campbell's "Hero With a Thousand Faces" archetype.

6. Other archetypal structures: universal human ways of being, the primal patterns we unconsciously adopt in creating our individual lives. Perhaps the Golden Rule is embodied in such a structure, and the 64 universal human situations that underlie the hexagrams of *The I Ching*. Jung felt that we inherit, genetically, a "collective unconscious" containing many powerful, universal, human archetypes. These archetypes do not forcefully direct and control. Rather, they are pre-established patterns, a few of which we may resonate with at any given time and make our own.

7. That executive, decision-making structure mentioned earlier, that consciousness-assisted brain process in which the system emergent we call *mind* affects certain physical subsystems and thereby controls behaviour.[17]

The specific ways in which these neocortical structures develop is determined largely by the array of influences that each person encounters, by each person's unique sequence of life experiences, by the culture in which each of us grows and develops. As Paul MacLean put it:

In the field of literature it is recognized that there is an irreducible number of basic plots and associated emotions. In describing the functions of the triune brain metaphorically, one might imagine that the reptilian brain provides the basic plots and actions; that the limbic brain influences the emotional developments of the plots; while the neomammalian brain has the capacity to expound the plots and emotions in as many ways as there are authors.

Anthropologist Ruth Benedict studied many cultures and, like the Existentialists after her, came to the conclusion that there was no one "given" human nature. There were many potential human natures, and each culture reinforced and developed a different mix of potential ways of being and behaving.

As I piece the story together from Maslow's account in *The Farther Reaches of Human Nature* and her book *Patterns of Culture,* Ruth Benedict noted great differences between the kind of people she found in one society and those she found in another. Some societies consisted of good, secure, likable, non-aggressive people. Others consisted of surly, nasty, aggressive people. The personality characteristics didn't correlate with any of the usual anthropological factors – geography, race, climate, wealth, etc. – and she struggled to find an answer. She found her answer in the type of reinforcement that particular cultures gave to ways of behaving, to attitudes, and to states of mind. She came to see human nature as a vast array of potential mind states and behaviours, with each individual's nature being determined to a large extent by the pattern of cultural reinforcements that the individual had experienced.

Some cultures reinforce the least desirable human potentials – those connected with our ancient brains: greed, hate, envy, etc. Our present North American cultures (and industrial cultures in general) tend to reinforce greed, and they reinforce violence in contexts such as war and some sports. They also emphasize the development of the rational mind and the development of capable players for culture-defined "worthwhile" activities.

Ruth Benedict and other anthropologists are telling us that we are clones of our culture to a much greater extent than we would like to think. Culture-originated brain programming determines much of what we do and how we think, yet we have great difficulty coming to see this.[18] Anthropologist Edward Hall has described the problem:

> There is, as far as I know, no way out of the dilemma of the cultural bind. One cannot normally transcend one's culture without first exposing its major hidden axioms and unstated assumptions concerning what life is

all about – how it is lived, viewed, analyzed, talked about, described and changed. . . . Bicultural people and culture-contact situations enhance the opportunity for comparison. Two other situations that expose culture's hidden structure are when one is raising the young and is forced to explain things, and when traditional cultural institutions begin to crumble as they are now doing. The task is far from simple, yet understanding ourselves and the world we have created – and which in turn creates us – is perhaps the single most important task facing mankind today.[19]

As Maslow's work showed, much also depends on how well our needs are met. When unmet needs are widespread within a culture, the effect can be particularly unfortunate. I live today in Prince Edward Island, Canada, but my Macdonald ancestors came from the highlands of Scotland. Coincidentally, so did the ancestors of many Prince Edward Islanders. The names Macdonald and MacDonald take up more space in my phone book than any other name. In addition, there are whole columns of Campbells, Stewarts, MacLeans and other Highland names. Like most North Americans, we Islanders tend to be interested in our roots, and to glorify our ancestors a bit. We take pride in being of Scottish descent, and like to picture our forebears as fine, noble human beings. At one point I read a bit of Scottish history involving my MacDonald ancestors. A story is told about how the Clan MacDonald of Glencoe invited the Clan Campbell to a feast in 1692. The Campbells turned on their hosts and slaughtered many MacDonalds. To get the gory details I turned to historian John Prebble's book *Glencoe: The Story of the Massacre.* I got more gore than I expected.

It turns out that the massacre was not an isolated incident. Life was hell for most Highlanders in the 1600s. Their rude dwellings were likened by people of the day to "cow-byres," "dung-hills," and "the earths of wild animals." During the winter their houses sheltered not only Highland humans, but Highland cattle as well. They were heated by open peat fires that filled them with smoke, reddening the eyes of people and cattle, and blackening the walls. Some smoke escaped through a hole in the roof. Some escaped through those holes in the wall they called windows.

Prebble gave an all too vivid picture of the pervasive brutality. Violence was part of life. Standard armament for a Highland man was two pistols, a dirk, a musket, a sword, and a bull-hide shield. Young boys spent part of each summer learning to use these weapons. Summers were the good times, but each winter brought the spectre of starvation. Life centred on making it through the current winter and preparing for the next. Summer activities included murderous raids on other clans, stealing cattle and anything else of value – insurance against the perils of the coming winter.

The barbarity of the Highlanders, it seems, was exceeded only by that of the English "justice" doled out by the King's man, the Earl of Argyll. Standard practice before hanging a man was to tear one of his arms from its socket and impale it on a pike. One of the Earl's lesser punishments was to bore a hole through a man's tongue with a hot iron. It was during this period that Thomas Hobbes called the life of man in the natural state "poor, nasty, brutish, and short." It was that in the Highlands.

Today on Prince Edward Island I, like my Highland ancestors, pass long winters and short summers. But no one is starving here. And murder and cattle-stealing are not standard pastimes. We blood descendants of those same violent clansmen live peacefully together, and treat each other at least as nicely as average North Americans do. The last time I checked, Prince Edward Island had the lowest per capita homicide rate of all Canadian provinces, and the lowest rate for all violent crime. Geneticists would tell us that the genes haven't changed appreciably in 300 years; three centuries is no time at all on the scale of evolutionary time. Yet there is this great difference between the behaviour of the Highlanders of the 1600s and the Islanders of today. Why? The answer, in Maslow's schema, is that the basic physical and psychological needs of today's Islanders are much better met. The answer, in Ruth Benedict's, is that today's P.E.I. culture does not promote violent behaviour to the extent that the Highland culture of the 1600s did.

If our physical and psychological needs are fully met by our society, if we live in a rich, stimulating, uplifting milieu, then it may be possible to actualize the very highest potentials inherent in those cortical structures. If our needs are not met, however, and if the influences we encounter do not motivate us to develop the best within us, then this won't happen. In the worst cases of deprivation, the person's inner experience and outer behaviour will be controlled much of the time by the mechanistic, reactive, hard-wired programming of the ancient brains. Also, whatever cortical capabilities we have developed are likely to be used to aid this reactivity.

We grew up in the culture we grew up in. We were indoctrinated with that culture's mores, values, and behavioural limits. Now, as we attempt to reduce our own reactivity to a much lower level, it would be foolish to expect a lot of help from that same culture. The setting of new limits and the search for ways of reaching those limits will have to be a personal matter.

As we have seen, a large body of research makes it clear that the reptilian and limbic brains come pre-programmed by evolution to generate "animalistic" behaviours and mind states. The great hope for us human beings is our extensive neocortex and its network of interconnections with the two ancient brains. Because of these connections, the human intellect has considerable control over reactive behaviour and mind states. On the negative side, the neocortex can *stir up* trouble. Thought and imagination (neocortical activities) are able to trigger reactive emotion and behaviour into existence. Thought and imagination also play a major role in *sustaining* reactive states. On the positive side, neocortical control of attention and energy can be used to bring reactive states to an end, and to prevent them from arising in the first place. The human "animals" among us are proficient at the first use of the neocortex; the saints and sages have mastered the second.

In genes/environment or nature/nurture terms, parts of human brains come genetically pre-programmed to initiate violent behaviour if those programs are activated. At the same time, other brain/mind processes – programmable ones, ones susceptible to influences from culture and environment – can prevent such triggering, at least in all but the most stressful circumstances. The frontal-lobe decision-making process can, via interconnections with the two animal brains, ride herd on them, monitor their outputs, and cut them off at the pass.

Even when the ancient brains are not determining our *actions*, intense mental reactivity sometimes arises and dominates consciousness. At such times the channel of reactive emotion takes over the screen of subjective experience. It may push everything else into the background, and can easily "ruin our day."

Have you ever watched the process by which these reactive mind states arise? Careful and persistent watching of what is going on in the mind can reveal it. It all starts with a reactive impulse – a kind of mental knee-jerk – arising, we understand, within a brain circuit that includes the limbic brain. It might be a pang of desire, jealousy, loneliness, or fear. Or it might be a flash of anger, hate, or lust. Sometimes it ends right there. Awareness may pick up the impulse immediately, and the thinking mind might respond with something like: "That's silly." Or, "That's inappropriate." Or, "I don't want to get into that." When this happens the whole thing gets dropped. The impulse occurs – triggered by whatever – but nothing happens to make a big deal of it. It's a bit like what happens in the following computer program:

```
1 PRINT "PANG OF JEALOUSY"
2 END
```

If you ran the above BASIC program, the words PANG OF JEALOUSY would appear on the screen once – and nothing more would happen. Frequently, what occurs is more like this next program:

```
1 PRINT "PANG OF JEALOUSY"
2 PRINT "Thoughts about why I should be jealous."
3 GOTO 1
4 END
```

In this example, the PANG OF JEALOUSY is followed by a little story – by a few thoughts about why I should be jealous. The story itself, the imagining, then becomes the cause for another pang of jealousy. It is handled in the program above by the command in line 3 to go back to line 1. If you ran this second program, the screen would fill with the two statements, then scroll indefinitely as the statements repeat over and over again. This scrolling would continue until you turned the computer off or reset it. The program never reaches line 4.

In computer programming it's called an infinite loop. In electronics and servo-mechanism theory it's called positive feedback. In everyday life it's called a *state* of jealousy. The isolated pang of jealousy leads to a story about it that leads to another pang that leads to more story, etc. The resulting state doesn't end until something interrupts the looping. The energy to keep it going might fail, attention might be drawn to something else, or new information might be received that convinces the mind to stop its painful foolishness. This, then, is the first step toward a non-reactive mental life, a life free of painful states of mind: **notice reactive impulses when they first arise.**

Once having noticed an impulse there are three ways of dealing with it – not all of them equally appropriate:

1. We can prolong the impulse by identifying with it and weaving a story around it, by feeding energy into a process that maintains it. If we do this, then a *state* of anger, fear, jealousy, or desire arises. This, in turn, may result in anger-based, fear-based, jealousy-based, or desire-based action of some sort.

2. Another option is to deny or repress the impulse – to push it into the subconscious. This is apt to have unfortunate consequences later, since repressed material is not really gone. It often returns and causes trouble.

3. A third option is simply to note the impulse, realize its automatic, mechanical, ancient-brain origin, and let it go.

Benjamin Libet has investigated the brain/mind process involved in making "voluntary" movements. His interesting results seem to apply to conscious decision-making in many situations – including our dealings with reactive impulses. The first of Libet's findings was that a conscious intention to move is initiated by unconscious brain processes. The evidence for this is a slow negative shift in the electrical potential of the scalp that precedes, by as much as a second, the arising in consciousness of an intention to move. If that strikes you as deterministic bad news, you'll like his second finding. Libet discovered that for a fraction of a second after an intention to act arises in the mind, a conscious decision can be made to veto the action. Thus, although the intention or impulse to act arises automatically, there is a brief, eleventh-hour "window of opportunity" during which conscious choice is possible.

Libet's results help make sense of some experiences of daily life. Did you ever find yourself pouring another cup of coffee without having consciously intended to? Did you ever brush a fly away or slap a mosquito "without thinking?" Did you ever get up from your chair and walk toward the kitchen – and only then realize that it was a pang of hunger that triggered the process? It seems that the unconscious programs of the brain initiate many actions, and if we're not attentive, we lose that brief opportunity to veto them consciously.

We can do nothing about the automatic arising of various thoughts, urges, and reactive impulses. Thus, there is no reason to feel guilt about any of them. It's all automatic – a product of mechanistic biocomputer processing. **Our humanity, our freedom, resides in the possibility that the conscious mind can assess and veto before the urge, thought, or emotion turns into mindless action.**

If we are attentive enough, then the discriminative, selective, human mind can say no to the mechanistic arisings, it can say no to the reactive perspective and yes to alternative perspectives. When the mind is alert and attentive in an allowing, non-reactive, broadly-focused way we can see feelings as simply feelings and urges as simply urges rather than as absolute imperatives upon which we must act. In this mode of attention, reactive impulses and other mechanistically-generated messages from our ancient brains simply represent more information – more input to awareness and to the final conscious decision-making process.

A quiet mind is the platform from which easy observation of mind contents is possible. By quiet mind I mean the state that exists when awareness is present but the level of informational activity is low – when there is little or no thinking, planning, remembering, fantasizing, or reacting going on.

What reveals itself in the absence of mental activity is our fundamental psychological state of being, the foundation of mind. It is a non-identified state, or if identification is present, it is identification with Being. It is a state of causeless happiness, a state of equanimity and energized but peaceful attentiveness. It is a state of desirelessness, contentment, and basic trust. It is a state of egolessness. It is a state in which the wanting and condemning psychological activities – reactive emotion and the intellectual tale-spinning that goes with it – have been surrendered. It is a state of psychological peace, coupled with a readiness to act out the promptings of Wisdom and Love.

The relationship between this still foundation of mind and its informational content is shown in Figure 6.1. The figure is similar to the appearance of an AM radio signal displayed on the screen of a laboratory oscilloscope.

FIGURE 6.1

MIND: AWARENESS MODULATED BY INFORMATION

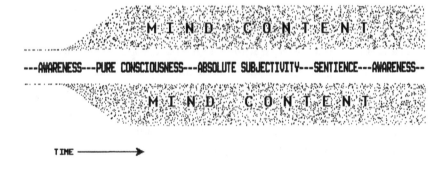

Always present is the pure informationless carrier, whether or not any informational modulation is present. A radio station's carrier is electromagnetic energy. Mind's carrier, or medium, or ground, is pure awareness: absolute subjectivity, consciousness without content.

The shaded area above and below the central band represents the informational modulation of the carrier. In the radio station example it represents programme content. Here it represents mind content – all types of mind content: the subtle emotions of being, intense reactive emotions, thoughts, fantasies, smells, sounds, sights, body sensations, the sense of time, the sense of identity, and memories. The amplitude of the mind-content modulation indicates, very roughly, the intensity of mind activity. In a perfectly quiet mind, the mind-content envelope would collapse and there would be awareness only.

Yes, underneath every noisy, reactive mind – supporting it, and enabling it to exist – is a quiet, peaceful, loving mind. Happiness is available to everyone, and right here. It seems almost too simple: Happiness, love, and peace simply *are* when reactivity and mental distractions are absent.

Most people in our culture look outside themselves for happiness, and for the causes of their unhappiness. Unhappy people try to modify the external situation until it gives them what they want. Somewhat happier people direct their efforts at keeping things the same; they are afraid that life's changing circumstances will take their happiness away.

Does this externally-oriented approach make sense? Think for a moment about what happiness is – your personal experience of it, and the circumstances under which you experience it. We speak of "moments of happiness," and our experience of happiness usually is momentary. When do the happy moments arrive in your life?

Mine often come just after some longing has stopped. Typically, I have been in a *wanting* state of mind. The wanting might have been intense or subdued, but I wanted something: To get a phone call from someone. To eat. To get a special piece of mail. Then that want suddenly ended: When the phone rang and it was the person I wanted to hear from. When I sat down to eat the meal. When I opened the mailbox and saw that it contained the mail I'd been waiting for.

We normally think that happiness results from pleasure. In looking carefully, however, I've seen that my happiness is connected not so much with pleasure as with the absence of desire, the absence of wanting. I'm happy whenever I don't want things to be any different from the way they are. In the examples above, happiness arrived right after the wanting stopped, but before the anticipated pleasure started. Happiness arrived before I actually began the telephone conversation, before I consumed the food, before I read the letter.

Happiness exists in that brief moment when the pain of wanting has stopped and the next pleasure has not yet begun. In that brief moment of freedom from reactive desire what exists is the primal background state: happiness, Being itself.

When we uncover this basic state we find that it has several aspects – mental, emotional and physical – and that certain qualities are attached to each:

The subjective state is characterized by alertness, attentiveness, awareness – a listening-like quality. Sensory perceptions are clear and distinct.

The intellect is inactive. The occasional thought may arise and disappear, but there is no discursive thinking going on.

Emotionally, there exists a quiet state free of reactive emotions like anger, fear, hate, wanting or craving, greed, envy, jealousy, etc. – except, perhaps, for occasional isolated impulses. Often, one or more subtle emotions are present, the emotions of Being: equanimity, loving-kindness, joy, wonder, peace or tranquillity, gladness, etc. A Hindu might speak of *ananda,* the bliss aspect of Brahman.

Physically, there is a state of stillness and peaceful readiness – free of agitation and the compulsion to *do,* but ready to act when Wisdom dictates.

Awareness, love, peace. It's what everyone is looking for, and it's right here at the core of each of us. Being feels like the fundamental basic me. When I allow myself to relax into that state I recognize it. I've often been there in the past without realizing it: When lying on a hillside watching the clouds go by. When doing something special for someone. When responding to the need of the moment without thinking – just organically doing what needs to be done. When watching a tiny baby settled into its place of being: aware, watching, peaceful, happy just to **be**.

Our culture doesn't tell us that this mental space is always available, let alone how to find it. It tells us to go for pleasure and settle for brief moments of happiness. It tells us to want a lot, and then satisfy those wants. It's a well-kept secret that happiness inheres in Being and is always available. It's not a secret in some circles, of course, but it is in the mainstream culture.

Wanting is one form of reactivity that disturbs our inner peace; anger is another. In North American culture, attitudes toward anger have differed from class to class, region to region, and era to era. Within my memory, the culture encouraged many of us – especially women and racial minorities – to repress anger. We were encouraged to deny it, to shove it under the rug of consciousness. Today, partly in response to the negative effects of that approach, anger has become acceptable – sometimes even fashionable and trendy. In certain activist circles, for example, if you are not angry about what your group seeks to change, you are not considered a true supporter. Anger can be a motivator, there is no doubt about that; that's why evolution built it into the limbic brain. But it is also a great disturber of inner peace – and there are other, equally effective motivators.

The wise ones have a secret: Anger just gets in the way. The Buddha likened anger to a burning coal that you are holding in your hand. Your anger hurts *you*. Anger is painful, and interferes with clear thinking and intuitive openness. The Dalai Lama has called being motivated by anger, "Very dangerous. Very risky." Vaclav Havel said that anger never played a part in his political protests. Even in prison, he was never angry with his political opponents or his jailers. Wise people don't need anger as a motivator. When they see from an intellectual and intuitive perspective that a situation needs to be changed, that is motivation enough. For them, anger serves no useful purpose, and they don't cultivate it. When impulses of anger arise they don't act on them or repress them. They take that third way: they note them and let them go.

We, too, can do it the wise way. We can defuse and transcend anger by broadening and deepening our view of the situation. We can ask what's really happening, and why. We can try to identify the impersonal forces at work. We can look for the troublesome values at the root of the problem, and attempt to discover how they became established and began to take control. By deepening our understanding in this way we deepen our compassion and our ability to let go of anger while at the same time gaining insights that will help us act effectively. Understanding transforms.

Happiness and inner peace are aspects of our root psychological state, they are not acquired. We don't find them through seeking and action.

Instead, we discover them through inward recognition and by letting go of emotional reactivity toward informational patterns that arise in the mind. Stillness is a choice that we make. It's always there. We could drop our wanting/hating attachment to mind content at any time. But we don't. We could detach, step out – and watch from that quiet, motionless centre of Being. But we don't.

Instead, we constantly seek. We try to improve ourselves, transform ourselves, make ourselves better. It doesn't accomplish what we would like, but our efforts at transformation eventually take us to the realization that seeking is a dead end. We seek until we realize that seeking is itself the problem. At that point a real transformation – a deep and effortless transformation – begins.

Happiness and pleasure really are two different things. It is possible to be happy even though experiencing physical or psychological discomfort. This happens after we have spent enough time in the quiet mind state. It happens when we start seeing things from a state of centred equilibrium, detached from the show. It happens when we start seeing ourselves as awareness, and the informational show as just a show. It happens when we start to disidentify with that show.

This detached, disidentified mental space is characterized by a nonchalant, take-it-or-leave-it attitude toward pleasure and pain. At some level, pleasure may still be preferred over pain, but it is now merely a preference, not a necessity. There is no compulsion to go after the next pleasure hit, and no compulsion to rid the mind of present pain. From this still, quiet vantage point the show is seen to be informational modulation, nothing more, it is seen to be simply a dance of differences. From this perspective we are able to accept whatever information is present without feeling compelled to change it or escape from it.

This vantage point is always here, always now, always available. Making a flip to this perspective in a lasting way comes when we arrive at the gut-felt conviction that it truly is the best possible vantage point: the sensible, positive, appropriate mental hangout. This normally happens only after many hours spent practising mental quiet, and numerous episodes in which we abandon the quiet for the seductions of the show.

CHAPTER

7

Seeing the Unity:
The Three Stages

This chapter and the next two deal with loosening our identification as separate independent personal selves, and deepening our sense of oneness.

First of all, why would we bother to do this? Would anything really be gained? Let's try to imagine what it would be like. Imagine, for a moment, that in every human mind the primal sense of identity did become identified with the ground of being. From that perspective, the unitive perspective, the perspective of Being, how would things appear?

For one thing, it would be clear that awareness simultaneously watches countless shows. It would be clear that I-We-Awareness watches these shows through billions and billions of sensory portholes. Part of the problem before was that the right hand never knew what the left was doing. Because occurrences of awareness seemed isolated and separate to human senses, the awareness at each window was fooled into thinking that it belonged to that window – and that window alone. It was fooled into thinking that it was separate from all other appearances of awareness. Now, from the perspective of Being, of oneness, it's clear that the awareness at each window is just another appearance of Being, the ONE. It's clear that all awareness, like all energy, is ONE in its intrinsic nature. It's clear that awareness is a universal, not a particular. It's clear that awareness is an aspect of the underlying medium, and not permanently attached or bound to any particular message.

With the sense of identity firmly attached to Being, death would be seen as just another aspect of the universe's constantly changing informational flux, not anything to fear. Yes, human bodies do eventually stop functioning. Yes, individual portholes do eventually go dark. Some windows go; new ones come. But from Being's vantage point it would no longer be the big deal it was when awareness identified with the window. Back then it was the *biggest* of deals. The loss of one window – when the sense of identity was attached to that window – appeared to mean total annihilation.

Dropping identification with a particular body/mind would transform our whole outlook. In letting go of the particular we would become free to see that we are everywhere, in every being. Shedding existing bodies and picking up new ones would seem as natural and right as the human system's shedding of 8000 stomach cells per second and the growing of 8000 new ones. By becoming unattached to any one window we would come to know – intuitively, deeply – that we look through them all. It would also be clear that we will continue to look and act forever more – in ever-changing, ever-new ways. As Joseph Campbell put it:

> Those who know, not only that the Everlasting lives in them, but that what they, and all things, really are is the Everlasting, dwell in the groves of the wish-fulfilling trees, drink the brew of immortality, and listen everywhere to the unheard music of eternal concord. These are the immortals.[20]

Identification with Being would bring about other changes too. Because the perspective after reidentification is long-term and holistic, war and the ecological rape of the planet would become absurd non-possibilities. The idea of localized short-term gain would lose its former meaning. Could centres of activity and awareness who look at the entire earth (and universe) as their body intentionally damage it? If you had Being's perspective, your concern would be the long-term well-being of the whole process. Your aim would be to actualize your highest values. Given that, you'd treat with utmost care and respect those rare special places in the universe, like earth, where conditions are favourable for that. Alan Watts apparently felt that this sort of shift in perspective is the only hope for those people with a control-the-environment outlook, the only hope for the man "saddled with the job of bending the world to his will":

No amount of preaching and moralizing will tame the type of man so defined, for the hypnotic hallucination of himself as something separate from the world renders him incapable of seeing that life is a system of geological and biological cooperation.[21]

However appropriate identification as a person might have been in the era of chance-enabled evolution, in this new era of mind-enabled evolution, it no longer is. Today, a shift to the perspective of Being appears not only appropriate, but necessary. **Pragmatically, widespread identification with Being would solve the most serious problems of person and world.**

In the first stage of the reidentification process we come to see all this conceptually, intellectually. We see that shifting from a perspective of separateness to a perspective of oneness makes rational sense. This is just the first step, however. We need to acquire the perspective of oneness, not just as a defensible intellectual position, but as a direct, personal, deeply-felt experience.

The overall transition seems to divide itself into three progressively deeper levels or degrees of reidentification which I'll call *intellectual, intuitive,* and *experiential.* To live in a totally reidentified way we need to move from the first, through the second, to the third. Fortunately, if our intellect comes to see the appropriateness of this identification it may prod us to head deeper. It may motivate us to take those additional steps that must be taken if we are to experience oneness intuitively and experientially.

We face a very unbalanced situation when we attempt a gestalt flip from our ordinary object-oriented view to the unitive or "Self-realized" view. As we've seen, many things work together to keep us solidly locked into the ordinary way of mentally ordering the world around us. We can, however, learn to let go of the person-centred view if we're earnest enough. Our best hope of doing it – of making the flip and reidentifying – is to do things that weaken identification with body and with mind contents, and do other things that strengthen identification with Being and the Whole. This is what we attempt in the *intuitive* stage of the reidentification process.

For most of my life I thought that religion and spirituality were the same thing. In my late teens I rejected organized religion, and because I equated the two, I also turned my back on spirituality. About age 40, I looked into the matter again. When I did, I saw that they weren't the same at all. Although the two had historically been linked, spirituality was independent of religion, and had always been there first.

I learned that each of the world's great spiritual traditions had several different modes of participation. Three of these predominated. I tagged them *Mainstream Religion, Fundamentalism,* and *Personal Spirituality.* I concluded that in Mainstream Religion, involvement was mostly intellectual and devotional. This was religion at the level of popular participation, the go-to-church level. Participants sought truth through an intermediary or intercessor – a priest or minister – who repeated and interpreted ancient teachings. Another feature of Mainstream Religion was that the religion's spiritual founder was revered, sometimes to the point of worship and deification. One advantage of this Mainstream approach was that it didn't require a lot of time. One disadvantage was that the knowledge gained was mostly intellectual, second-hand knowledge. Often, people were not able to run their lives by it. The Mainstream mode was, for many people, superficial.

The mode of Fundamentalism was similar to the Mainstream mode but less intellectual; involvement tended to be experiential and emotional. For anyone immersed in science, however, there was a big problem. In Fundamentalism, ancient religious texts were interpreted literally, and some of these teachings clashed with what is accepted as real and true by science and the culture-at-large. This resulted in a kind of cognitive dissonance, a mental discomfort. The individual was told to resolve this by having faith in the literal teachings, by believing them completely, and by denying the truth of the scientific/cultural view. What got lost if you took this approach was openness to other viewpoints, and openness to changing your own. Fundamentalism seemed incompatible with an open, reality-seeking attitude – one in which you held your working hypotheses lightly and tentatively.

The third mode was the one that interested me. It was the mode of the founders of these spiritual traditions – the mode of first-hand, direct investigation. It is also a mode that is alive and well today. I discovered that each of the great spiritual traditions had – and to some extent still has – its "mystical" branch devoted to personal exploration. In the early centuries of Christianity there were Gnostic sects involved with direct "transcendent knowing," and during the Middle Ages there were Christian mystics who sought the direct experience of truth. Even today there are comtemplative orders of Christian nuns and monks. Quakers, too, have their first-hand approach: sitting silently, attempting to sense "the Light within." In Judaism it's Kabbalah. In Islam it's Sufism. Hinduism has Vedanta and its many yogas. And there are direct-participation practices in Zen, Tibetan, and Theravadin Buddhism.

In this third mode, the mode of personal investigation and discovery, the objective is to see through the veil of everyday reality to a deeper underlying reality, a reality of oneness. Each tradition offers a set of techniques to help the individual accomplish this. There are Hindu mantra and "I AM" meditations, Buddhist breath meditation, the riddle-like koans of Zen, the mind twisting stories of the Sufis, and the sweat lodges of native North Americans.

I saw that in these direct practices the object was to find out for yourself. You didn't have to take anyone's word for anything. You needed no intermediaries. And the only faith required was enough to try the practice for awhile. Also, this approach actively encouraged open-mindedness and a reality-seeking attitude.

The ancients spoke of Spirit. I'm pretty sure that the reality behind their term Spirit is the same reality that lies behind my term Energy-Awareness. Spirit, or Energy-Awareness, is the root, heart, foundation and source of all physical and mental vitality. It is the ground of life, function, and perception. And just as I have come to see Spirit in contemporary terms, I also see spiritual practices in contemporary terms. Legitimate spiritual practices are really psychological practices. Their aim is to allow human beings to understand the game of existence more clearly, to help people reach the point – psychologically – where they see holistically and adopt holistic ways of acting in the world. Personal spirituality's lone negative seems to be the time and effort required. An hour each Sunday isn't going to do it.

Particularly helpful in the *intuitive* stage of the reidentification process are practices that help loosen identification with the personal self and strengthen identification with the ALL or the ONE. That kind of practice regime shifts the balance of mental influences, increasing the likelihood that a temporary "gestalt flip" of intuitive recognition or reidentification will occur. There are other names for this kind of event. Some have called it Self-realization. Others, Enlightenment, or Liberation. Whatever we call it, the person experiences a shift of perspective that allows the underlying unity to be seen in a thoroughly convincing, intuitive way. In some cases the seeing is so deep that a temporary shift of identity occurs, and Being is directly experienced as one's universal Self.

Unfortunately, the presence of the normal ego, plus other influences, prevent this gestalt flip from occurring easily. Gut-level identification with Being requires gut-level disidentification with the small-s self. Unwilling to let go, to give up, to "die," the intellect tenaciously clings to the old *self* delusion. As we will see, loosening that tenacious hold involves insight, acceptance, and abandonment rather than any kind of seeking and finding. It is, after all, simply a matter of seeing clearly what already is.

In the final *experiential* stage of deepening, we move from flashes of insight about oneness, or short visits there, to setting up residence. If you're familiar with those ambiguous, reversible figure-ground pictures in the psychology books (or Salvador Dali's or M. C. Escher's work based on that principle) you know that you can't always flip with equal ease between the two visual possibilities. This is often the case when you first encounter a new figure, and even more so if you're not told in advance that there are two ways of perceiving it. The stairway-cornice figure may look stubbornly like a stairway for instance. Or you may see only the old woman in the old-woman/young-woman picture if no one tells you about the young woman possibility. You soon learn, however, that once you've seen the less obvious possibility, it's easier to see it the next time. And if you practise switching back and forth from one perceptual gestalt to the other, switching usually becomes easy – even though you had trouble at first.

That is analogous to what happens in the *experiential* stage of reidentification. After the first reidentification experience you continue your disidentification/reidentification practice. Then slowly, gradually, the likelihood of flips into the new mental space increases. Eventually, some degree of control over the process develops.

A few people have reached the point where they experience oneness permanently. One of these was Vedantist teacher Sri Nisargadatta Maharaj. In the passage that follows (recorded some forty years after his first gestalt flip) he shares his view of things:

> I see as you see, hear as you hear, taste as you taste, eat as you eat. I also feel thirst and hunger and expect my food to be served on time. When starved or sick, my mind and body go weak. All this I perceive quite clearly, but somehow I am not in it, I feel myself as if floating over it, aloof and detached. Even not aloof and detached. There is aloofness and detachment as there is thirst and hunger; there is also the awareness of it all and a sense of immense distance, as if the body and the mind and all that happens to them were somewhere far out on the horizon. I am like a cinema screen – clear and empty – the pictures pass over it and disappear, leaving it as clear and empty as before. In no way is the screen affected by the pictures, nor are the pictures affected by the screen. The screen intercepts and reflects the pictures, it does not shape them. It has nothing to do with the rolls of films. They are as they are, lumps of destiny, but not my destiny; the destinies of the people on the screen.[22]

Before such a state arises permanently, or can be attained at will, it happens in discrete episodes. Several of these are described in William Bucke's turn-of-the-century book *Cosmic Consciousness*. The following are more recent accounts. The first was written down during an hour-long episode of identification, the second immediately after a three hour episode.

> The feeling of I and me is the same as it always was, but that feeling no longer seems trapped within the body. There is space, detachment. The I or me watches the body go through its motions, washing the dishes one by one. The body is perceived as a detached machine, a sophisticated robot performing duties in accordance with prior programming – being viewed from somewhere apart by *me*. I am aware of its mental workings too – it's like having a readout attached to the robot's biocomputer. The robot itself doesn't need the readout. It gets its instructions straight from

the computer: "Grasp the dish. Lift the dish. Place the dish. Et cetera."
It's just that I get to peek at the robot's mental life like a voyeur – I get to
see some functions of its biocomputer. I saw the intention to do the
dishes, for instance, and before that, the desire to eat lunch.

And concerning the second:

I moved into an unfamiliar mental state. It was as though a cloak of concentration and mental stillness had descended on me. It was not at all like
my usual distraction-prone state in which part of me would want to go
off fantasizing about the future, part would want to linger in the past, and
part would search for that elusive knife-edged ridge called the present. It
was as though that narrow ridge had opened up wide and provided me
with a stable place in the present moment on which to stand. The world
looked the same, but it was here, now. All those moving, searching parts
of me had come back together. I was in the timeless present moment.
Psychological time stood still. Also, everything I perceived was perfectly
acceptable. The present moment was perfectly okay just as it was. There
was nothing worth grasping, nothing that needed pushing away, and
nothing too subtle to be interesting. It was a totally satisfying place to be.
I also had a strong sense of oneness, a sense that everything around me –
trees, sky, ground – was also me. I thought: "I am surrounded by my
universal body. It's all just part of the Big Me."

With forty years of practice, and not many demands put on the problem-solving rational mind, it should be possible to stay in the reidentified
mental space continuously – as Nisargadatta apparently did. For active
Western people, however, the optimum is probably to return automatically to the reidentified space after each excursion into intellectual activity. Then, reidentification rather than fantasy or memory becomes the
natural resting place for attention – our new mental "neutral."

We humans appear to be the first creatures on earth with any hope of
understanding our existential situation. We're on the ragged edge. We
have sophisticated scientific instruments with which to explore the cosmic message, but we may not be much better off than the dolphins and
whales when it comes to realizing our true Self as cosmic Medium. Like
the minds of other animals, our minds are still rooted in reactive emotion.

And we still identify the primal sense that "I exist" with the body/mind. It's possible for a human being to make the gestalt flip of reidentification, but for most people it's not trivially easy.

Identifying with Being involves seeing through or seeing past the space-time frame of reference – that frame of relativity and difference that is information's home. It involves finding a new frame of reference, an absolute frame: is-ness, identity, oneness. Perhaps the ocean/wave metaphor can help. Picture the broad Atlantic ocean and two waves, one near the coast of England, the other near the coast of Nova Scotia. With our usual space-time frame of reference we visualize two separate things or events. Off the coast of England is one wave of a certain size and shape, occurring at certain co-ordinates of latitude and longitude, at a certain instant of time. Twenty-five hundred miles away, at another instant of time, and other co-ordinates, is a wave of a different size and shape. We can picture each wave mentally, and if we had all the numbers we could describe the two separate things or events in great detail – using terms of time and space.

Waves are ocean seen from the space-time frame of reference. But there is another frame of reference or point of view: that of the ocean itself. From ocean's perspective there is only ocean – the oneness of ocean. Waves are not separate things, they are ocean. Their shape and location and timing are all unimportant within this second frame of reference. Their identity as ocean is the important thing here.

From the space-time point of view, Being can be intuited as the medium that is waved or formed or patterned by information. But from its own point of view, Being – like ocean – is timeless and placeless. It just IS, a ubiquitous oneness. We are that Being. And by learning to let go of the space-time frame of reference – that sometimes pernicious point of view which obscures oneness with the illusion of thingness – it is possible to discover our own deeper identity, and experience the world from the perspective of oneness. Like the ocean, we are everywhere. We are the awareness that watches the show in every mind, the energy that enables every action, and the love that envelops it all.

CHAPTER

8

Seeing the Unity:
Disidentifying

This chapter, and the next two, deal with some of the techniques – the psychological or "spiritual" practices – that help us move into that more holistic space, that allow us to see and evaluate all this for ourselves. The problem I face in attempting to write about these things is a universal one: incompleteness. There are as many paths to wisdom as there are wise people. Also, there are many time-proven, effective practices – many more than one person could evaluate first-hand in a lifetime.

There is yet another problem. On any path to wisdom there are one-time-only events: flips to new perspectives, flashes of insight, etc. You can't undo these insights; you can't un-see. When you've intuitively realized something, you're no longer the same. You can't have that first-time realization again. This makes it impossible for one person to compare, first-hand, the relative effectiveness of even two practices; you're only naive once.

What writers on spiritual practices normally do is to share their experiences, and their feelings about the limited range of practices they have personally encountered. That is what I will do, here and in the following chapters. If I've missed a better practice – perhaps the all-time best practice ever – sorry, but someone else will have to write that book.

Some things that help to start or deepen the disidentification process are serendipitous. One of these is misfortune. Being out of control helps to break down the assumption of infallibility, the assumption that "I" am controlling what happens. The alcoholic who admits that he can't control his drinking has taken the first step toward sobriety. Humiliation sometimes has a similar effect. The failure of some ego-sponsored venture, or shame at some moral lapse, helps destroy the assumption that "I" am always right. These things can weaken the ego and adherence to the ego-centred view.

The approach of death can help too. Seeing the "dark at the end of the tunnel," as Gail Sheehy put it, is bound to make "me" question existing assumptions of control and continuity. This doesn't mean that we must wait for adversity or the onset of middle age. We can adopt today, if we wish, intentional practices which weaken the forces that keep us seeing things in the same old ways.

Early in my inner journey I read several of J. Krishnamurti's books. Krishnamurti focused on the human situation and avoided cosmological speculation. Neither God nor an all-inclusive Self were a necessary part of his worldview. His central concern was the mess that the human mind makes of things, and I later came to see him as a spiritual psychologist of the first order. Seeing what the mind is up to was his goal, and mindful attention to its workings was his method.

Krishnamurti felt that the starting point for upgrading our inner lives was seeing with clarity what's going on in our minds. We needed to pay close attention to mental events as they happened. Only then could we do anything about them. He spoke of a pathless path that starts and ends here. The sort of advice he gave us was this: Watch what's going on in your mind. See the mischief that thought creates. See the danger of it as you would the danger of a poisonous snake in your path. Then simply stop thought unless it is necessary for some legitimate purpose.

I tried to take his advice but found that I couldn't. The problem, as I see it now, is that most of us ordinary people have not developed the skill at attending that Krishnamurti, over the years, had developed. Although his prescription is correct, his directions call for a bigger first dose than most people can tolerate. The giant step that Krishnamurti asked us to take is beyond us.

If we look elsewhere, we find that there are baby-step practices which –

if followed earnestly enough for long enough – will develop the clarity, quickness, detachment, and persistence of noticing necessary to see what needs to be seen. There is, in other words, a practical route to Krishnamurti's goal.

Another reason that Krishnamurti's goal is not easy to reach is that the ego or small-s self doesn't really want us to be aware of what the mind is up to. Again and again we delude ourselves into thinking that we've cleaned up our mental act, only to discover that we've still been pushing some not-too-pleasant truth about ourselves under the rug of consciousness – denying it, or repressing it. The classic defense mechanisms of Western psychology – denial, repression, projection, rationalization, displacement, and intellectualization – are all ways in which we lie to ourselves about mind contents and processes. Defense mechanisms crop up daily in each of us, shielding awareness from some aspect of the truth about mental goings-on.

Would-be reality-seekers become effective, practising reality-seekers when they discover for themselves the extent to which they have been blocking their own view, when they begin to cut through that smoke screen of defense mechanisms. The classic Western way of doing this is to undergo psychoanalysis or some other form of psychotherapy. And this may be exactly what's called for if we have persistent feelings of insecurity, difficulty relating to others, or an abiding sense of low self-worth. If, however, the problem is rooted in existential distress rather than psychopathology, there is another way. It turns out that the same sort of baby-step practice that helps develop steady mindful awareness also helps develop the detachment to see what the defense mechanisms keep shoving out of sight. The form of this practice most familiar to me is called Vipassana, Insight, or Mindfulness meditation. (Vipassana means insight in the Pali language.) It is the practice I encountered at my first meditation retreat back in 1977, the retreat I mentioned in the Preface.

Mindfulness practice does an end run around the defense mechanisms. When you earnestly practise watching mind contents in an honest, non-judgemental, reality-seeking way you start to see through the smoke screen. You say, "Ouch!" when you do, because what you see differs from what you'd like to see. But at a deeper level you're glad, because you know that seeing what *is* opens the door for transformation to take place. As Krishnamurti never tired of pointing out, human minds are a mess. And it is only when the individual sees that mess clearly that the mind can (and will) undergo a radical cleanup – the radical transformation that he advocated, and that you and I want.

I'm not a Vipassana teacher, or a Buddhist, but I'm convinced of the power for change inherent in the practice. I refer in Chapter 14 to information about Vipassana retreats, and to several excellent books by Vipassana teachers. I know of no better sources of information on the subject than these books. I would, however, like to give you my "student's perspective" on the practice, based on my own experience with it.

Vipassana is easy to practise in the home situation. To begin you simply sit, close your eyes partly or completely, and pay attention to the subtle sensations that accompany breathing. Students are usually given a choice. You can pay attention to the sensations that the air creates as it enters and leaves the nostrils. Or you can pay attention to the sensations that accompany the rising and falling of the abdomen as breathing takes place.

At first the meditator will be doing well just to keep the attention at the chosen location for a few breaths, let alone pick up subtle nuances. Lesson one in the mechanical nature of mind comes quickly – when you realize that attention has drifted away from its object and off into thought. That lesson is taught and re-taught countless times as attention drifts off and is brought back to its intended object. At other times sounds or strong body sensations will capture attention. Whatever the distraction, you're encouraged to note what is happening, let it go, and return your attention to breath sensations.

Because what sounds so simple turns out not to be, the tendency is to get discouraged and angry. Learning to be gentle and forgiving toward that poor old body/mind takes some time. It also takes time to realize that this drifting off will happen again and again and again. (The Buddha once told a man that if only he would be continuously mindful for seven days he'd become fully enlightened. I wonder if the statement has ever been tested.) The task is to be patient and understanding with that poorly-programmed brain. As one Asian teacher pointed out, this practice requires infinite patience. The practice also helps develop it.

Most teachers feel that the more time spent doing the sitting practice the better. One or two sitting sessions per day of 45 minutes to an hour in length are typical of established "at-home" practices. It sometimes takes a while to work up to sitting for an hour. This is particularly true if the individual is bothered by physical restlessness, or has a strong negative reaction to the discomfort that is often present. Most people have never before tried to sit perfectly still for more than a minute or two. The body does eventually adjust and settle down – but like the mind, it also needs training. A typical recommendation is to start with whatever length of time you're able to sit, and gradually extend the time until you can sit still for an hour.

Intensive Vipassana retreats involve the same basic practice (plus variations), but the continuity of practice and the supportive environment lead the meditator to deeper levels of exploration. Perhaps telling you a bit about my own first retreat will give you some sense of the experience.

The retreat was held at the Insight Meditation Society's centre near Barre, Massachusetts. The facility was formerly a Catholic seminary and struck me as perfect for the purpose. There were enough sleeping rooms to house a hundred retreatants and a volunteer staff of twenty. The chapel, with pews removed, made an ideal meditation hall. And there were other large rooms suitable for walking meditation. The grounds were spacious – with 80 acres of woods, and room for a large vegetable garden. The woods were filled with 150- and 200-year-old trees, and laced with stone fences built by the early colonists. Along with everything else the place *felt* right – it had a peaceful, meditative atmosphere.

I was uneasy about doing this first retreat. I wanted to learn to meditate, and my attempts at home had been frustrating. But 12 days? All day? Every day? I arrived late in the afternoon on the appointed day, and after checking out my assigned room and taking a tour of the facility I headed for the library. There I began talking with a young woman who was back for her second retreat. Her first one sounded like a disaster. She'd had many personal problems at the time, she said, and once her mind started to get quiet she had begun to cry. After three days of crying she left the retreat. That was more than a year before. Since then she had spent time in Bangladesh with the Peace Corps, and was enthusiastic about doing another retreat. Her story didn't exactly ease my jitters, but on the other hand, here she was, back again.

After supper we carried our pillows, cushions and other sitting paraphernalia into the meditation hall and found places to settle in. The introductory talk covered the rules and procedures as well as the daily schedule during the retreat. We were told that the wake-up gong would sound at 4:30 a.m. At 5:00 we'd start an hour of sitting meditation. Breakfast would be at 6:00. We'd eat the main meal of the day at noon, and have fruit and tea at 5:00 p.m. There would be a 45-minute talk on some aspect of Buddhism each evening, and bedtime was scheduled for 10:00. Almost all the remaining time would be filled with meditation. Most of the sitting meditation sessions would be an hour long, with half-hour sessions of walking meditation sandwiched between. The food would be vegetarian, and we would have an interview with the teacher every other day. Silence was the rule except during teacher interviews, and both reading and writing were discouraged.

As demanding as the routine appeared, it made sense. The object, as I saw it, was to quiet the mind. Not only would talking disturb other people, but it – and reading and writing as well – were left-brain activities. If we wanted our noisiest brain hemisphere to quiet down it was just logical to stop doing those things. I decided to follow the rules, and did so except for the many notes I eventually scribbled in my pocket notebook.

After receiving the instructions on breath meditation we practised for an hour – a sobering hour. As I had discovered in my few attempts back home, what sounded so simple wasn't. There was a veil of fuzziness between me and my perception of the breath – sort of a film or fog. And I found sitting still, for even a few minutes, uncomfortable. This retreat wasn't off to the easiest of starts, but as I headed to bed I resolved to give it my best effort.

The fuzziness continued all the next day and most of the day after that. I found the breath subtle and damnably hard to keep my attention on –

which is no doubt why it made a perfect object for training the attention. Again and again my attention would wander, and again and again I would bring it back to the breath. There was a gradual improvement as time went on, but no dramatic breakthrough until late on the second full day of practice. Suddenly, the sensation in the nostrils began to interest me. This dull, boring, stupid sensation that was so elusive had suddenly become *interesting*. This breathing phenomenon – so much a part of our existence that we rarely notice it unless a head cold interferes with it – had risen from the ground and become figure: an entity capable of engaging my interest. For the rest of that evening – and the pre-breakfast sitting the next morning – the interest and clarity of perception remained, and I could keep my attention on the breath for many minutes at a time.

We'd been warned that overeating would interfere with the practice. The meals were delicious, however, and eating was one of the few sensual pleasures left. As a result, I pigged out that morning on yogurt and stewed prunes, freshly baked dark bread, a banana, and herbal tea with milk. At the next sitting I found the fuzzy fog back again. My attention tended to lapse, and I was on the verge of dozing off.

Lunch was even harder to resist than breakfast: sliced tofu stir-fried with bean sprouts, peppers, celery – and served with rice. There was also a salad of spinach and sliced mushrooms with a light coating of creamy dressing. Under protest from my appetite I went light on the amount, and by mid-afternoon the clarity was back. Something had helped.

Sitting for long periods many times a day was not fun. There were knee pains and back pains and pains in the butt. I did everything I could think of to maximize my comfort, and tried all three of the basic sitting options. Most people sat cross-legged on an mat with their backside supported by a high round cushion called a zafu. They used the zafu with traditional yoga postures like the lotus and half lotus, or worked out their own variations. Other people used a semi-kneeling posture, with a small wooden *seiza* bench supporting their weight. Still others sat on a conventional chair. I tried them all, with every possible variation of cushion, pillow, and foam mat. I gave up on the zafu – it was just too uncomfortable – sort of like papa bear's chair. The ordinary chair, on the other hand, affected me like mama bear's. It wasn't physically too soft, but whenever I sat on one my mind got soft and sleepy. In the end, I settled on the seiza bench. It was "just right" as the story goes. The need to support my own back kept me more alert than when I used the chair, yet my knees were under less strain than when I used the zafu.

Our teacher encouraged us to lengthen our sitting periods if possible, and to avoid moving for as long as possible whenever we sat. Having exhausted every *external* way of increasing my comfort I started experimenting with some of the internal ways that the teacher suggested. Focusing attention on the painful sensations was sometimes helpful. It helped my concentration to build, and the pain would sometimes lessen – or even dissolve completely at times. Occasionally I'd be able to sit for an hour and a half without moving my legs or rear end – but that was rare. There were also times when nothing worked, times when the pain burned so strongly in the knees that it was impossible to sit still. But I kept trying.

The first side effect of the meditation involved my dreams. Either I had become better able to remember my dreams, or I was dreaming much more than usual – perhaps both. There were flying dreams and travel dreams and fearful dreams. The meditation practice seemed to be thinning out the barrier between my conscious and subconscious minds.

Soon after, I saw that this thinning of the barrier was not just a nighttime effect. At about six days into the retreat, insights of various kinds started bubbling up from my subconscious. These were *Aha!* and *Eureka!* experiences similar to those I'd encountered when solving engineering problems. In situations when I'd had a problem to solve – one requiring a non-obvious, creative solution – I would gather facts and try with my conscious mind to solve it. Sometimes this rational process would lead to an answer right away, sometimes it wouldn't. At times I'd gather data and wrestle with the problem for several days without success. I didn't get too uptight in these situations because I'd learned that my subconscious mind was also trying to solve it. After a period of struggle, I'd put the problem aside and get a good night's sleep. Then, possibly in front of the mirror the next morning, Eureka! – the answer would come. It arrived from somewhere in complete put-together integrated form.

In my experience, two conditions had to be met before this other mind would produce creative insights. First, I had to have fed the intuitive process enough data. Second, the problem and its answer had to be meaningful to me. The quieting of the mind in meditation didn't seem to eliminate either of these requirements, but it did help the process to work. It became clear that the barrier normally present between the conscious mind and this integrative process perforated more readily during and after prolonged meditation. I began to experience moments of sudden intuitive knowing – moments of deep gut-level insight.

These retreat insights were not solutions to pressing problems, but they were answers nonetheless. They seemed to relate to, and arise from, the endeavor to grow and understand that I'd begun back in the mid-1960s. Every book I'd read since then, every significant conversation I'd had, and every new wonder I'd experienced was raw data stored away somewhere in memory. What seemed to happen was that my subconscious mind, at some deep level, began fitting those bits and pieces of data together in new patterns and arrangements. I began to get at least partial answers to some of my questions about what our existential situation is all about.

I can vividly recall the first of those big insights. It was the afternoon of the sixth day. I was strolling around the building between sitting sessions, getting the kinks out of my legs, when I noticed an amaryllis in full bloom. There were many flowers and plants around, but that big, showy, horn-shaped white flower seemed worthy of special attention. I sat down close to it and peered into the bell of the horn. The flower's entire structure seemed dedicated to reproduction. The pistil, awaiting pollen. The pollen-coated stamens, standing erect. The hood-like petal, both protecting those parts and advertising their presence to passing insects. I thought about the flow of life from seed to seed and the plant's involvement with sun, soil, water, insects, and other "external" factors. Then it struck me: what I was gazing at was not a flower *in* the universe. It was a flowering *of* the universe.

A realization of connectedness and oneness swept over me. I sensed the oneness of the whole mental/physical process we call Universe. And I sensed some sort of upward impetus or life-force behind it all. I saw individual flowers and people as ephemeral manifestations of the ongoing process, temporary events that mark and define the present state of that process. An individual amaryllis is a sometime thing: its life product a few seeds and the atoms of its structure – all to be returned to the earth. It is a temporary centre of activity in a much larger process. I saw the process itself as the one basic ongoing entity.

I felt blown away by all this, and the excitement lingered. It was clear that many answers to fundamental questions are right in front of us. The problem is that we don't see what's there to be seen because we almost always look with a noisy, distracted mind, and are almost always driven by some purpose. Here I was looking with no purpose, and with a quiet mind, and I was seeing. I felt that the artist in me had opened up. These were deeper, clearer, more real perceptions – freer of stereotypes and cultural assumptions.

When that first retreat was over, I felt that it had been the most difficult experience of my life, and the most rewarding. Watching mind contents from morning to night, day after day, is hard work. Sitting for long periods is uncomfortable. But in the retreat environment things do happen much more quickly than in an hour-a-day practice at home. The situation itself facilitates movement toward that gestalt flip. Many activities that reinforce the "ordinary" view have been removed: There is little (if any) talking. You don't read. You're temporarily freed from problem-solving and other intellectual challenges. In fact, you don't have to *do* much at all. What is reinforced is mental quiet and paying attention to subtle stimuli.

I don't think it's necessary to *start* mindfulness practice with a retreat, but because our normal industrial-culture lives are so busy and buzzy, occasional retreats do seem a necessary part of serious practice. Retreats are also where the teachers are, and while we don't need a teacher forever, it is helpful and reassuring to have some guidance in the beginning, and from time to time along the way.

This practice – especially in a retreat environment – undercuts mainstream culture's domination of our minds. So much of the magic wrought by meditation (and just plain solitude) comes from the dying-away of reality-masking influences such as language (structure and vocabulary), the consensus-reality perspective, and other cultural influences. Withdrawal from those influences, coupled with heightened awareness or "paying attention," combine to give the individual a fresh look at the old world. The world is seen more directly, and we become aware that culture-spawned categorizing and interpreting has been hiding important aspects of reality.

The first thing that typically occurs in Vipassana practice is that the mind starts to quiet down. (Again, this is especially evident after the first few days of an intensive retreat.) If we try to tell ourselves to stop thinking it probably won't work. If, however, we direct attention to some object other than thought – to the sensation of the breath at the nostrils, for example – thinking eventually subsides all by itself.

The first "events" worth noting result from this quieting of the rational, verbal mind. They are what often occurs with any type of meditation – including mantra meditation. I refer to the bubbling up into consciousness of previously subconscious stuff. Facts and impressions that we have suppressed or repressed often arise when the mind gets quiet. We start to have psychological insights – insights connected with the way we are currently living our lives. Sometimes, too, there are insights about the past, and sometimes remorse about the unskilful, unhelpful ways we've acted in the past. It's a bit like psychotherapy – except that it's the quiet mind that brings significant material up into consciousness, not the questions of a therapist. Such insights can have therapeutic value, of course; regardless of what triggered them they can lead to changes in our behaviour.

Other early insights are what I might call existential or cosmological insights – insights into what is going on and what it's all about. My amaryllis experience was one of these. Some people have them – particularly those who are seeking answers to existential questions as I was – others don't. Like the psychological insights, they arise because the mind is at long last quiet, not because mindfulness has improved significantly.

If your mind is one of those busy, buzzy ones, and you do not yet have open communication between your intuition and intellect, your first quiet-mind experience might possibly be as dramatic as mine was. For many others, it would not be. Clearly, my intellect had not been in the listening mode for years. The intuitive process had lots to tell it, and was not going to let this rare opportunity pass.

Another thing that happens when the mind gets quiet is that intuition and intellect start working together in harmony. Our deepest, most satisfying knowing occurs when intuitive and intellectual knowings agree, when there is a concept or mental model to fit the feelings, and a feeling of intuitive rightness to accompany the concept. The models and metaphors of our rational mind give form and detail to the intuitions of the guts. Also, flashes of intuitive insight help us internalize – truly see and accept – those intellectual models that fit, and flesh out, our intuitions. Understanding in the deepest and fullest sense is not a matter of intellect *or* intuition – it's a product of the harmonious congruent meshing of intellectual models *and* intuitive insights. Intellect is a facilitative process, and just as intellect can help the limbic brain pursue its reactive goals, so intellect can help intuition pursue its holistic ones.

As you continue to practise this sort of meditation, mindfulness gradually develops. Mindfulness is careful noticing. It is being able to see what is happening in the mind. It is being aware of what you do as you do it. It is noticing what the body/mind does as it interacts with its milieu. As the mind starts to adopt mindfulness as a habit it begins to have the type of insights that Insight Meditation is really all about – insights into the nature of the mind/body process. We start to see for ourselves the things that Krishnamurti and many others have told us are there to see.

What a difference seeing for ourselves makes. It makes ALL the difference. Intellectual knowledge is like a tentative hypothesis. We believe it to a point, but only to a point. Eventually, we begin to see for ourselves: "Yes! This *really is* the way it works!" Then the intellectual knowledge moves from the head to the guts. It becomes our personal wisdom. It is totally convincing, and we comfortably base life decisions on it.

If the practice is continued, mindfulness eventually develops to the point where reactive impulses are regularly seen in the impulse stage – before those impulses become full-blown states of mind. The brain's decision-making process then has a tremendous amount of leverage in dealing with them. There does not seem to be any way to reprogram or retrain the brain to prevent totally such impulses from arising. But if the individual has internalized the value of not turning reactive impulses into reactive mind states, then the brain can take steps not to start the "story" that converts the first into the second.

This is the stage when Krishnamurti's kind of looking at last becomes possible. You look, and when you have seen the damaging chain of events for yourself – possibly for the 200th time – you begin to "see the danger." It starts to seem positively nuts to continue to crave, or get angry or jealous. It becomes apparent that all this pain is being created needlessly. Mindfully noticing our unskilful, unhelpful, unpositive ways of thinking, emoting, and behaving is all that is necessary to start the transformation process. Nothing else needs to be done.

Prolonged mindfulness meditation also fosters disidentification with the show in consciousness. *Acceptance* is one of the factors at work. The meditator practises accepting the contents of the present moment, whatever they are. Because this is the opposite of I-type behaviour, this acceptance of what *is* slowly, gradually, undermines the "I." We can look at this as the dying away of a bad habit. Identification with body and mind contents is to some extent a mental habit like other mental habits. It is a well-entrenched habit, but one that can at least be weakened by not exercising it. When we non-judgementally watch mind contents, egoic activity dies out. When we just look and accept, identification weakens. The mind then moves closer to the point where a gestalt flip of disidentification/reidentification is possible.

Simply becoming still, both physically and mentally, also changes the balance of mental influences and moves us toward the point where a flip to that other gestalt can occur. During prolonged sittings, awareness watches mental event after mental event happen automatically – the whole show being created by unconscious brain activity. There is constant movement and change in the mental display. A moment may come, however, when awareness becomes aware of awareness – when the observing faculty becomes aware of itself as an entity separate in some sense from the show, and different in nature. At such moments it becomes clear that awareness is inherently still and unchanging, and that all motion, all change, resides in the informational show. Stillness of body as well as mind seems to help this sort of realization to occur.

English is not a language that allows us to describe the complete relationship between awareness and the show in one short sentence. As a result, you may still find the matter confusing. At times I speak of awareness and the informational show as being separate – and from one perspective they are. But from another perspective they are not. Perhaps an analogy will make the situation clearer. If you tune across the FM broadcast band with one of the older receivers you hear a loud hiss between stations. In our analogy this hiss corresponds to nothingness, to no reality at all. When you tune to a station's frequency the hiss disappears, and if there is no programme at that moment there is silence. The energy carrier that the station sends out corresponds to Being – still, quiet, but powerful and enabling too. What it enables is the transmission of the programme, the show. The show modulates the carrier (changing the carrier's frequency in FM, or its amplitude in AM). The physical reality is the carrier itself; the show is a changing informational pattern encoded in the instant-to-instant changes impressed upon the carrier. The show and the carrier are separate conceptually; they are different kinds of reality. At the same time, they are one in the physical reality of an energy carrier undergoing modulation. Similarly, awareness and the mental show are conceptually different kinds of things, and in that sense are separate. They are one, however, in the reality of awareness undergoing modulation.

Careful noticing allows us to avoid much pain. Disidentification allows the pain that remains – the unavoidable pain – to stop being a big deal. Once the identification with mind contents is broken those contents lose their power to manipulate and coerce and limit the actions of the body/mind. That power comes directly from identification – from the belief that they are me. Once the body/mind no longer believes that, their power is gone. At this point we see just a churning biocomputer spitting out an incredible mixture of helpful and unhelpful information – as it always has. We see that even the big bugaboos like fear and jealousy are just harmless information-coated energy. We become free to settle back into our true cosmic identity, watch the informational show, and BE intuitive wisdom.

CHAPTER

9

Seeing the Unity:
Identifying with Being

Meditation on breathing-connected sensations (the first stage of Vipassana) is the beginning practice in all three major Buddhist traditions: Theravadin, Zen, and Tibetan Buddhism. Vipassana remains the central practice in Theravadin Buddhism – also known as Hinayana Buddhism. This Buddhist tradition emphasizes disidentification. In the Theravadin view, disidentification is all that is needed for liberation from suffering. The show, the melodrama of existence, is seen as unsatisfactory process. We humans identify with aspects of the show – particularly with mind contents and with the body – and this delusive identification, or "wrong view of self," is a primary contributor to our suffering. Liberation results from seeing at a deep level that there is nothing tangible we can call a self, that there is just this impersonal process going on.

In Zen Buddhism, Taoism, Christian mysticism, and the Advaita Vedanta tradition of Hinduism the aim is not only disidentification with the body, but reidentification with the ONE, with Mind-essence, with the Tao, with God's Being, with Atman/Brahman – with the *ground of being*, whatever the label. This is the *perennial philosophy* way of looking at the world. I understand that Aldous Huxley didn't originate the term, but his book by that name popularized it. The essence of the perennial philosophy, in his words, is this:

> The ground in which the multifarious and time-bound psyche is rooted
> is a simple, timeless awareness. By making ourselves pure in heart and

poor in spirit we can discover and be identified with this awareness. In the Spirit we not only have, but are, the unitive knowledge of the divine Ground.[23]

The ideal in the perennial philosophy traditions is to see that one's true Self is the ground of this world – see it intuitively, experientially, deeply. Once we have seen that, our task is to live the life of a person in this world – but live it from this inwardly liberating vantage point. In Self-realization, Nirvana (the cosmic medium) and Samsara (existence) are seen in their proper relationship as aspects of the cosmic ONE. Individuals liberated through reidentification are not dominated by, lost in, or controlled by the show of everyday life. Still, almost all are eager to make a contribution to it, to serve the higher purposes of the process.

Just as there are activities that facilitate disidentification with the body/mind, there are also activities that strengthen identification with Being, and with the process as a whole. One practice of this kind involves paying silent attention to the basic sense that we exist. This has been proposed as a primary practice by Vedantists like Nisargadatta, and by the anonymous 14th century Christian who wrote *The Book of Privy Counseling,* and *The Cloud of Unknowing.* Nisargadatta called it meditation on the *I AM* sense, meditation on the basic sense of being. The Christian author described it as paying attention not to how or what we are, but to the subtle feeling *that* we are. In this practice I make the object of attention the subtle intuition that I exist – not the form which that existence takes, but the primal fact, or sense, or reality of existing.

Early in 1980 I did a five-week retreat in my apartment, and devoted it to this practice. I found the practice highly effective. It helped create psychological distance between mind contents and the primal sense of identity, and led me to associate that sense of identity with Being. I will describe one of the key happenings during those five weeks – not because anyone will repeat it exactly, but because it illustrates the kind of door-opening event to which intuitive-stage practices can lead.

During periods of sitting meditation, I settled into, and got familiar with, the basic sense of self – that fundamental sense of existence or basic identity, the *I AM* feeling. It was a comfortable mental space, and the mind got quiet just as it had whenever I watched breath sensations for a prolonged period.

By two weeks into the retreat my mind had become very still and quiet, and I became aware of subtle changes in the quality of feeling connected with this experience. I noticed that each time I settled into the *I AM* mental space it felt a little different. I then noticed that the difference had something to do with where my attention rested, and how broadly it was focused. If my attention happened to settle on the chest/heart region, I tended to have loving feelings. If it settled on a muscled area like an arm or shoulder, then the sense of being, or self, had a warm quality. If attention came to rest on the stomach, it felt slightly heavy, in that "heavy meal" sense. If attention broadened out to include the whole body I experienced happy feelings, a kind of quiet joy.

One morning I started to play with this, moving the focus of attention around, and noting the changes in the sense-of-self experience. I gradually moved the focus upward, stopping to feel each sensation along the way – chest, neck, lips, nose. I continued to move awareness upward, little by little, until finally it was directed at the inside of my head. When I reached a certain point in this transition the body-sensation components of the sense of self disappeared. The basic sense that "I exist" became almost completely free of content, free of sensory modulation. It was close to no experience at all, close to a pure void, almost nothing – **except I knew that I was still intensely aware.**

I saw two things at that moment. First, there really was a pure awareness free of content. Second, since I had moved my sense of self slowly, gradually to where all sensation vanished, what was left – pure awareness – was obviously the true home of that sense. This manoeuvre had caused the last thing that was not "me" to fall away. There was nothing left but pure awareness staring into a void containing only that low-level visual sensation that always exists as a sort of irreducible background noise. Direct experience had confirmed for me what perennial philosophy teachers had been saying for centuries: The true "me" is awareness itself. The words of Nisargadatta again:

If I ask you what is the taste of your mouth, all you can do is to say: it is neither sweet nor bitter, nor sour nor astringent; it is what remains when all these tastes are not. Similarly, when all distinctions and reactions are no more, what remains is reality, simple and solid.

And:

Give your heart and mind to brooding over the "I am," what is it, how is it, what is its source, its life, its meaning. It is very much like digging a well. You reject all that is not water till you reach the life-giving spring.[24]

Those physical sensations I experienced when awareness focused on the body provided subtle content for the "I am" experience. But the nature of that content changed as attention moved from one body part to another. Only one thing was always constant, always present: awareness itself. When awareness shifted to an almost sensation-free place it became obvious that my basic identity was the one constant factor: pure awareness – that which remained when the physical sensations were not. The life-giving spring.

My earlier concept of unity was a unity of process. All the specifics in the universe were part of one big specific – the total process. It was a horizontal kind of unity. Now I intuitively saw another kind of unity, a vertical unity in which the myriad specifics were all one with the underlying general. It was the unity of interpenetration. The eternal medium of Being interpenetrated, supported, and allowed the everchanging message of form and function to exist. And my true identity was the medium itself.

I wrote: "The perceived world looks the same as it always did. It's just that there is now this cognitive sense that Being underlies everything I perceive. It's a sense of the depth of things, a sense of the attributes of things, of Being, of capital-S Self permeating the old view. Life, awareness, organic wisdom, and love are seen in a new way. They are no longer seen as isolated events, but as the all-pervasive reality poking through the illusion here, there, and everywhere. I sense the reality of the medium and its values in a way I never did before."

I reflected on my basic sense of being or selfhood always having felt basically the same whether I was four or 44. My subjective self had always felt ageless. I now saw that the real me *was* ageless. I was the same timeless universal awareness that had watched the cosmic show since t=0. For the previous 44 years it had been taking in the view through the Cop Macdonald porthole. The same awareness – identical in quality, universal in nature – also watched the show in countless other places. For the first time in my life I felt really close to animals. That was my true Self watching the show in the cat's head and everywhere else.

I also realized that I was more than awareness. I was the life that animates the body/mind, the energy that makes life possible, and even the mass involved in every body's structure. I was these and other intrinsic qualities of the universal medium of existence. I was the eternal ground of being in all its aspects. Existence, the universe – the whole cosmic show including the Cop Macdonald body/mind – was an ephemeral media event, a modulation of Being. I, Being, was the source of the cosmic show and its audience. I interpenetrated this ever-changing display and was its changeless foundation. I was the permanent medium; the universe was my temporary message.

I thought about humanity. We human beings were deluded gods, lost in the drama, taking the game too seriously – sucked in like fans watching a movie or a football game. Identification with the body/mind was the prison. Detachment. Mindfulness. Awareness. Those were keys to the prison door. Once we stepped through the door we could see that our true identity was the one ground of being that gave rise to the game. At that point we could choose just to Be, and watch – or choose to get involved in the game again with a caring detachment that allowed more daring and effective play than ever before.

As that retreat ended, the metaphor that came to mind was one of ascent. All my life I had been climbing a hill, and as I climbed, my field of view had gradually enlarged. I had spent time reading and travelling and having a great variety of experiences – and as a result, my view of what *is* had gradually become broader and more detailed. Since I never wanted to miss anything, I'd always kept my eyes on the ever-growing view of the valley below. Then, during that retreat, I turned around, away from the valley and toward the hill itself. Instead of finding myself just facing the hill, I discovered that I was now able to peer over the top and see what was on the other side. I saw that there was another valley on that side: the realm of Being. I experienced a sudden step-function increase in my appreciation of what there was to see and explore. I was not yet living in that other valley. I didn't know it in intimate detail. But I now knew beyond any doubt that it was there.

In one way it was like taking in a whole new view. But it was also like suddenly discovering an incredible unseen richness in the old view. In the old view – the science-based view – Being was unacknowledged, buried within phenomena. This older view was still there, but I could now see Being as a separate added dimension. I was beginning to see, as Lawrence Durrell put it, "Between the lines, between the lives."

An intuition-based flip to another way of seeing things – such as that just described – is typical of the sort of insights that mark this intermediate, intuitive, stage in the process of reidentification. When something like this happens you start to take the unitive perspective very seriously. Even though you return again to more ordinary ways of looking at things, you are never quite the same. You've been there. You've seen things from this other perspective. It's a bit like returning from a trip to New York or some other exciting city. The experience itself is over, but you don't forget what the experience was like.

Meditation on the *I AM* sense is not the only practice that weakens personal identification and strengthens identification with the ALL or the ONE; there are many others. I've tried several of these in my daily-practice situation, and found them helpful. Most would be called spiritual practices, but let's look next at one that doesn't have that label. It originated in the camp of Western psychology, and is called Open Focus.

Some years ago I read a book that prepared me to be interested in Open Focus. It was the reissue of a book first published in 1936 by English psychologist Marion Milner – written under the pen name of Joanna Field, and titled *A Life of One's Own*. It is the story of Marion Milner's inner journey. The part I found most interesting was her discovery of a wide-focus mode of paying attention. She had always perceived life around her in our ordinary narrow-focus way where attention is automatically shifted hither and yon by personal interests and desires. Then she discovered that if she could watch with no purpose to fulfil, or desire to meet, that she could not only pay attention to everything happening now, but she became completely happy. When she was in this open, accepting, wide-focus mode – watching her experience with detachment – she felt happy, connected, no longer alone. In the stillness that accompanied this mode she got clear intuitive messages about what to do, how to live. Her book spoke to me.

A year or two later I ran across Open Focus, and recognized it as a structured technique for attaining the mode of attention that Marion Milner described. Open Focus was developed by a Princeton, New Jersey group involved with biofeedback therapy. I sent first for their book: *The Open Focus Handbook,* and then for their series of cassette tapes. The tapes are designed to talk the listener into the Open Focus mind state: "a state of effortless awareness in which no one element of simultaneous experience is focused upon or weighted more heavily than any other part." This description was remarkably similar to Marion Milner's description of "wide-focus attention." But there was one important difference: Marion Milner just accidentally ran across this state, and for a long time she had trouble finding and entering it at will. The people who developed the Open Focus exercises had worked out a practical method of leading a person to it.

Another practice involving elements of both disidentification and reidentification is the set of exercises called "dis-identification exercises" by Roberto Assagioli, and described in his book *Psychosynthesis.* The basic idea is to repeat to yourself short clear statements about the existential situation – statements that make sense to you intellectually but which you have not yet fully internalized. The practice involves mentally repeating these statements, perhaps at the beginning and end of each session of sitting meditation, and whenever else during the day it occurs to you to do so.

Using Assagioli's basic approach, I came up with some statements of my own – using the terms and concepts that speak most clearly to me. I repeat to myself statements like:

I am awareness watching the show in consciousness.

This local body is not me, but is part of my universal, informational body.

These mind contents are not me, but are an informational show created by the functioning of the local brain.

Throughout the universe I am the energy that enables, supports, and activates. And I am the awareness that watches.

All physical structure and all mental experience is but information, a transient modulation of my eternal being.

I'm not trying to absorb someone else's ideas when I do this. I have known – first intellectually, and later intuitively – that they describe a legitimate way of looking at what *is*. I practise in this way to help make this perspective my ordinary everyday perspective.

Can you see the similarity between this practice and detaching from a scary movie simply by reminding yourself that you're in a theatre, watching patterns of light on a screen? Whenever I'm in a theatre and do that, the movie immediately loses its power to affect me. In my version of Assagioli's practice I remind myself that I – universal awareness – am situated in the theatre of the brain, watching the informational show that the brain projects. Reminding myself of this reduces fear and other intense emotions. I realize that even if this brain should be destroyed, I-awareness, the true me, will still be watching the show in billions of other theatres.

This intellect-based practice probably won't, in itself, cause a gestalt-flip of reidentification. Still, it reinforces other practices and helps keep them on track. It's a verbal reminder of the reality that exists here and now, the reality lying behind the obscuring show of everyday life, the reality we're trying to comprehend – not only intellectually, but also intuitively and experientially.

Generosity is a practice that was strongly advocated by both the Buddha and Christianity. Christianity's message to care about others always made ethical sense to me. But I now see that there was more to it than that. Adopting an interested, caring attitude – and actually giving of ourselves and our means – is a reprogramming exercise, an exercise that leads to changed mind-habits, to new internalized values.

Acting in caring ways toward other people can move us closer to seeing the unity. Love is Being reaching out into the informational world – receptive love as interest and acceptance, and active love as compassionate, harmonizing, upleveling action. Practising interest, acceptance, and compassionate action – even when done imperfectly – makes them more deeply real to us. Acting in these loving ways helps dissolve the illusion of separateness between the local self and the object of its love. Love recognizes oneness – if not explicitly, at least implicitly.

Closely related to acting in generous, caring ways toward others is thinking kind and generous thoughts about them. When we forgive others who have harmed us, and wish them happiness and the best that life has to offer, we are training our own mind to identify with other people – to feel less separated from them, to feel more closely connected with the process as a whole. There is, in fact, a formal Buddhist lovingkindness meditation in which we forgive ourselves and others. We send thoughts of lovingkindness to ourselves, those we love, and those who we have not yet come to love. Sending out warm wishes to others may or may not help them, but that is not the point. The primary reason for doing the practice is to weaken our own egocentricity, and strengthen our feeling of connectedness with other beings.[25]

A related approach is to practice looking outward in a more general way: To immerse ourselves in a study and appreciation of nature, for example. To develop a sense of wonder. To surrender to the greater wisdom, to what *is*. Albert Einstein advocated this broader sense of love as an approach. You'll recall his statement quoted earlier:

A human being is a part of the whole called by us universe, a part limited in time and space. He experiences himself, his thoughts and feelings as something separated from the rest, a kind of optical delusion of his consciousness. This delusion is a kind of prison for us, restricting us to our personal desires and to affection for a few persons nearest to us.

Einstein didn't stop there. He also gave his prescription for action:

Our task must be to free ourselves from this prison by widening our circle of compassion to embrace all living creatures and the whole of nature in its beauty.

We might call Einstein's way *the way of interest.* It is possible for watching or observing to be just a surface kind of activity. Genuine interest, however, leads to a penetrating kind of observation that takes us to deeper levels. Interest wants to go to the heart of things, to truly understand.

I've noticed that interest brings mental quiet with it. Interest is a state of mind in which the brain co-operates with primal awareness. Interest clears the decks, if you will. It stops the smoke screen, the garbage, the unnecessary, and lets awareness be aware, with few impediments. When interest is present the brain turns off competing mental activity, doesn't it? When we are interested, the brain does all it can to heighten awareness. We might say that interest is awareness with all the help a body/mind can give it. Interest has an active, curious, investigative, probing quality. It is awareness coupled with, and amplified by, a desire to know, to understand, to be clear about what *is*.

Interest is particularly beneficial when the mind gets interested in the mind – in its activities and contents. Most of us, most of the time, are unduly influenced by our self-images – often by the ideal self, by the person we want to be. We get so caught up in the image of the person we want to be that we lie to ourselves about the person we are. We needn't be ashamed of doing this. There is no "I" doing it. Our present programming just makes it happen. But it's not an ideal situation. We cross an important threshold when our interest in seeing what *is* – in seeing the truth beneath the facade – exceeds our need to avoid it and sweep it under the rug of consciousness. To put it another way, the threshold we cross is one of coming to love our small-s selves enough to be honest with ourselves. Or, in Gandhi's terms, it is coming to value Truth above all – or at least above our desire for psychic comfort.

To the extent we are able to explore this realm honestly, with intense interest and a heartfelt desire to know, we find that the very act of exploration changes things. In physics, observing the behaviour of an elementary particle affects that particle's behaviour. Similarly, when we explore some emotion or physical sensation with a keen interest in understanding it, we find that this deep exploration transforms the thing we're interested in. Observed closely – microscopically, acceptingly – it's no longer what we thought it was during those distant glances when we were trying to push it away.

When we are in a state of intense interest, and are not thinking, there exists a whole and appropriate responsiveness of the body/mind to the situation. When thought is out of the way, and interest is present, the body automatically acts in fitting ways. Interest stirs up latent energy which energizes both the watching, and the action that comes out of the watching.

Interest is both the goal and the method. It is difficult at times. Interest is never a lean back and take it easy state. It must be constantly renewed, moment to moment. It's never a tuning out. It's always an intense, still, tuning in. Acceptance of what *is* is an integral part of interest, isn't it? If I watch with interest what is going on in the moment, I am accepting it. If I turn my attention away in an attempt to avoid, I am not. Being interested – compellingly, totally interested – is being in the present moment. Practising interest – making an effort to observe mind happenings with interest and acceptance – is the way to get there. We must love truth to approach life this way, to follow this practice. Yet if we are earnest, the practice will lead to an interest in all, a love for all.

Both Alan Watts and Da Free John have advocated happiness as a practice. Free John created a formal practice based on observations about happiness similar to the ones I made back in the "quiet mind" part of Chapter 6. Free John takes the position that happiness is our fundamental state. We don't realize this, however, because we are taught from an early age that we should only allow ourselves to experience happiness at certain times, under certain agreed-upon conditions. We are taught to seek happiness, or to seek those circumstances where – according to the culture's rules – it is right and proper to feel happy. The truth is that happiness inheres in Being and does not require any external events at all for its arising. Thus, we don't have to wait until the "right" external circumstances arise to enter the mental state of happiness.

The practice of happiness is founded on the observation that we are happy when we don't want anything. We are happy when we're in that quiet place of Being.

Alan Watts quoted Oscar Wilde as saying: "When I am happy I am always good, but when I am good I am seldom happy." It's true. When we are happy, don't we tend to be more loving and considerate than when we are not? When we adopt "good" behaviour just because we think that we should, very often we are not happy. This all makes sense once we understand that happiness is fundamental, and that the Being place is not only the happy place, it is also the place of love, attention and acceptance. Thus, if we connect with this primal happiness we also become connected with the other aspects of Being.

Acceptance is a good example of this. Does it make sense to you that happiness and acceptance are almost the same thing? Doesn't remaining happy, no matter what, rest upon accepting, no matter what? If this is true, then we have a choice. We could practise acceptance or we could practise happiness. Practising acceptance is a little tricky. Unless our practise is completely whole-hearted, acceptance can acquire a sort of stoic, grit-your-teeth, effortful, even self-righteous quality; that "I'm being good" attitude can arise. Such feelings and attitudes get in the way. By practising happiness it's possible to skirt around this possibility. Being surrendered to happiness is likely to happen effortlessly. And once happiness has been allowed, acceptance is there too.

A similar thing happens with sensitivity. We could make an effort to be more sensitive to other people and the natural world. Or we could just accept the increased sensitivity that comes as a natural side-effect of being more deeply happy.

Happiness also brings with it what amounts almost to a protective shield against fear and other forms of reactivity. Happiness serves as a natural barrier to our own mentally induced hell in all its varieties. When firmly situated in Being's vantage point we stop pushing away unpleasant informational inputs and simply watch them.

The first step in Free John's practice is to convince yourself of what he calls this "lesson of life," namely, that happiness is a prior or fundamental state associated with Being, and is not anything you can attain by chasing after it. As he put it, "You cannot become happy, you can only be happy."

As I understand Free John's practice, it is similar to Vipassana, but Vipassana in which the whole body is taken as the chosen field (or object) of attention. When you do this the subtle emotional colouration that arises is the feeling we know as happiness or quiet joy. Putting it another way, you allow attention to widen until it includes the whole body, you allow the release of all wanting and seeking, and you relax into ever-present, ever-peaceful Being. The state in which you then find yourself is happiness.

Simply letting go of all wanting and seeking (surrendering the ego) leaves you in a mental space of unalloyed happiness. Ego will raise its head from time to time, stirring up wants of various kinds, but if you are firmly in the habit of keeping attention and the whole body sense together in this place of happiness, then wanting and seeking are just more stuff passing by.

Free John's formal practice has three elements:

1. Understand the process through which unhappiness arises. (See for yourself that unhappiness arises through non-acceptance, through seeking for something other than what *is* at this moment.)

2. Feel into the always-present happiness and allow attention to remain there.

3. Ask at random: "Avoiding Relationship?" (Existence is characterized by unbreakable interconnection, by unitive relationship. But the ego denies and avoids this, heading off on its own desire-based narcissistic adventures.)

Free John's many works deal with this practice, especially *The Bodily Location of Happiness* and the book he wrote under his former name (Franklin Jones) entitled *The Knee of Listening*.

The *Open Focus, I AM,* and *Happiness* practices are similar. I'm almost tempted to call all three the same practice – with slight differences of nuance. There are, in any event, several common characteristics:

1. All three practices are marked by a high degree of attentiveness.

2. Attention is in the wide angle mode that includes the whole body, and opens outward beyond it.

3. All three are marked by letting go of wanting. By surrendering in some sense. Wanting is replaced by just watching, just accepting – by contentment just to be.

In all three practices attention is normally kept wide – wide enough to include the whole body – and this keeps us aware of that basic sense of existence, or happiness. At the same time, it allows us to see all the "stuff" that the brain keeps churning out. As this practice is continued, awareness/Being/happiness is seen increasingly to be the primary or core me. And all that informational "stuff" appears increasingly secondary and superficial.

CHAPTER

10

The Path to Wisdom

In Chapter 7 I referred to three progressively deeper levels of re-identification: *intellectual, intuitive,* and *experiential.* Here I'd like to apply these same terms to three sequential stages in the process of becoming wise.

Although I call the first stage the *intellectual* stage, it is also a stage of need-meeting and general preparation. It is the stage of life during which our basic needs are met – the physiological, security, belongingness, and esteem needs – Maslow's "deficiency needs." If these needs are not adequately met during this period, we're held back. We're not totally free to follow the path that goes beyond them – and are not likely even to be drawn to it.

Gail Sheehy, Sam Keen, and others who have commented on the stages of adult life, have noted that this period is characterized by exploration and experimentation. Starting on our teens, and on through our 20s and 30s, we explore the informational world. We read. We think. We act. We travel. We experiment with life. I did it; you did it or are in the process of doing it. As we pass through this period of our lives, we find some answers. Just as important, however, we load our memories with data for future processing. To the extent that we live this stage actively, the stored data will be there in quantity. To the extent that we live this stage attentively, it will be there in quality too.

Later in life – often during the 40s or 50s – the youthful illusion of immortality ends, and for many people culture-sanctioned games like *career, consumption,* and *status* begin to lose their appeal. Some people at this point feel the need to move on to a more meaningful way of being. They undertake an inner journey, a trip of psychological/spiritual investigation and development. In doing so they enter the *intuitive* stage of their growth toward wisdom. I don't mean to imply here that *only* older people decide to take inner journeys. These days, increasing numbers of people in their 20s and 30s are also doing it. Some do it instead of adventuring outward; others include it as part of a mixed bag of adventures. It will be exciting to see how all this works out. Do you share my guess that unless too much of the usual kind of personal development gets left out, starting early will prove much better than starting late?

In the intuitive stage, the barrier between the subconscious and the intellect gradually thins. Communication between intellect and intuition is established, and a mutually beneficial relationship begins. Solitude, psychotherapy, and meditation are all aids that may be called upon to help this occur.[26] Once the communication starts, beneficial things happen. For one thing, unconscious junk – previously repressed and denied material – may again become conscious, removing its ability to block movement forward, and allowing it to be dealt with. For another, the intellect opens to the advice and problem-solving activities of that take-everything-into-account intuitive process. Then one begins to have those intuition-born insights and gestalt flips – those mental **Aha!** experiences through which we rebuild our worldview from the inside out.

The worldview we formed in the intellectual stage arose from an outside-in process; it was the product of perception, intellect, and cultural training. The brain took in data from the outside world and, for the most part, ordered it in conventional culturally-sanctioned ways. In contrast, our new worldview arises from an inside-out process; it is the product of quiet-minded flips to more holistic ways of seeing, and our own intuitive reshuffling and re-viewing of decades of data. The intuitive stage is a stage of enlightenment and re-visioning, a stage when Maslow's "peak experiences" occur more frequently than before, a stage in which the brain/mind begins to interpret old data in new ways.

The label *experiential* in the final, *experiential stage* does not refer to having new life experiences at this stage of life, which is usually the 50s or later.[27] It refers instead to the deeply experiential way in which the world is encountered at this point via the newly-acquired perspectives. This is the stage for a final housecleaning, for leaving the last vestiges of reactivity behind, for living wisely from day to day. It is the stage for becoming an agent of noumenal creativity – a channel through which holistic values become manifested in the world. It is the stage for moving from intuitive flashes of self-realization toward a continuously experienced gut-felt reidentification with the whole process and its ground, for moving from transient peak experiences to Maslow's ongoing "plateau experience." The idea of "becoming all I'm capable of becoming" takes on a new meaning at this stage. In the intellectual stage of growth it meant actualizing our personal potential to the very limit. Now it means actualizing the highest potentials of the universal process.

There is a paradox: On one hand we are there already, it's just a matter of seeing that. On the other, there are many things that interfere with seeing what must be seen. One wall of the room in which I'm sitting is covered with books. In many of those books some spiritual teacher tells the reader that everything necessary for the most radical kind of personal transformation is already there within the person, just waiting to be activated the minute we see our existential situation as it truly is. I've read words like those many times. I would generally say, "Yeh. Exactly!" And then keep right on looking outside myself for the answer.

It *is* all there. We simply have not yet developed our powers of attending to the point where we can see exactly what is there – and perfectly obvious – when observed under the right conditions, from the right perspective. Fortunately, there are those simple, dumb-seeming, stupid-seeming things we can do to develop that ability.

To learn to play a cello or a piano well there is a whole array of skills that we must acquire. Here the task is simpler, but just as arduous. There is really only one skill needed: Call it mindfulness. Or bare attention. Or careful, continuous, non-judgemental awareness. Or non-identified noticing. Whatever we call it, the time and effort required to master this skill are similar to that required to master a musical instrument. Ken Wilber compared the total task of reaching Self-realization with that of getting a Ph.D. Beware of those who promise shortcuts and fast results! There is no shortcut, no easy way. When it comes to playing the piano, or learning to type, or getting a Ph.D., we accept this. But we still keep looking for some shortcut to becoming a wise, free, and loving person. Does that make sense?

There is a way of looking at spiritual practices that may help us better understand their role in all this. I refer to *The Rule of Ripening*. The rule is this: You choose to practise now, with effort, what you eventually hope will be your effortless, natural way. As you practise, you gradually "ripen." You slowly move toward the time when the fruit of insight and Self-realization is fully ripe and suddenly drops. It is this ripening process that we work on in the *intuitive* and *experiential* stages of practice.

While ripening is a helpful metaphor, *rebalancing* is perhaps a better fit with our image of the gestalt flip. We could say that spiritual practices help shift the "gestalt balance" so that a flip is more likely to occur. Look at it this way: The influences we encounter in normal living are heavily weighted toward keeping us locked into the ordinary perspective and point of view. If we spend 100 per cent of our waking time in this mode, then the likelihood of flipping to that other perspective is very small. If, however, we modify our mode of living, and spend six or 13 or 19 per cent of our waking time (one, two, or three hours a day) in practices that pull us toward that other view, then the probability shifts. If, in addition, we attend an occasional week or ten-day retreat during which we spend 100 per cent of our time in such a practice, it shifts even further. For decades, you and I have been conditioned to interpret perceptual data in the ordinary, culturally-accepted way. Given this, it's not surprising that we must practise another way of seeing for awhile – quite awhile – before it becomes our natural way.

Ripening and rebalancing are useful ways of conceptualizing the role of spiritual practices. Another is E.F. Schumacher's concept of *adequatio*, or adequateness of mind. "The understanding of the knower must be adequate to the thing to be known," said Schumacher in *A Guide for the*

Perplexed. In his view, the role of spiritual practices is to develop this adequatio, or level of adequateness. Piaget, the great student of child development, pointed out that there are whole classes of concepts that are meaningless to a five-year-old. We could say that the five-year-old does not have the necessary "adequateness of mind" to comprehend them. Spiritual practices help adults develop the adequateness of mind for wisdom and holistic kinds of understanding.

There are a few people who seem to have been born wise and caring, or who developed wisdom at a young age as the result of special life circumstances. The rest of us need psychological/spiritual practices: to ripen us, to shift the gestalt balance, to develop our mental adequateness. Ruth Benedict, you will recall, pointed out that our outlook and behaviour depend largely upon which of a broad range of potentials are reinforced and strengthened by the prevailing culture. Fortunately, we're not prisoners of the culture into which we were born. We can change our personal situations in ways that alter the balance of influences to which we expose ourselves. We can try to create a friendly, supportive micro-culture around ourselves. We can adopt a spiritual practice, and practise – with effort – being the ways we effortlessly want to be.

Reading has been a helpful element in my practice, but it's a potentially dangerous one. For years reading *was* my practice, and that just doesn't work. Books are great for acquiring intellectual information of many types. They can also be guides of a sort on the spiritual path, but no more than that – no more than signposts pointing the way or maps giving a rough description of the territory to be explored. The exploration itself must be first-hand and experiential, direct and immediate.

As Krishnamurti put it, you have to see for yourself. You can read the words over and over again, but without first-hand experience to connect the words to, they don't really sink in. You must see what is going on in your own mind, in your own actions, and in your own relationship with the immediate situation. Intellectual hearsay and reports from others won't do. Mind must see for itself, through its own direct experience. The words make perfect sense after you've been there, but the words alone won't take you there.

That being said, books are still useful in all three stages as motivators and clarifiers. They are a helpful influence – a needed element in that microculture we're trying to set up around ourselves. Tapes of lectures and retreat talks are worthwhile for the same reasons.

I often spend the last half hour before going to sleep reading Nisargadatta, or Krishnamurti, or one of half a dozen others. These are true knowers of reality, and the books of such people bear countless readings. It's exciting to re-read them because as my practice and understanding deepen I see more clearly what they were getting at, the truths to which their words point. Old passages will often sparkle with new clarity. And sometimes I'll run across wonderful, illuminating passages that I never remember seeing before. Yes, books are valuable at all stages of the process – but you can't read your way to inner freedom.

It not only takes great patience to enter the intuitive stage of the process, it also takes great courage. For one thing, we must be willing to dive deep and face the unknown truth about what the badly programmed brain and its mind are up to. We must be willing to cut through our self-images. There is much fear connected with that. Still, it is only if we are courageous enough to see the reality of what *is* – see the greed and hate and anger and fear and loneliness – that escape from their domination is possible. Today we are confused, and despite our heartfelt wish to be free – and earnest efforts to become free – there is part of each of us that wants to stay blind to the present patterns of mind and action. Mindfulness reveals all that needs to be revealed for that freeing transformation to take place – if we practise it diligently enough and long enough. But before we can deal with the considerable trials of practice, we must first overcome our fear of starting.

The fear that keeps people from trying meditation is the same fear that keeps them from seeking counselling and psychotherapy. They sense that there is something of a tangled mess in the mind, and they would dearly love to have it all untangled. But they resist the obvious: To untangle a tangle you have to look at it, to see clearly the present tangled state. With the seeing of what is tangled, and how, there is the hope of freeing it up – almost an assurance of freeing it up. Keeping the tangle in the dark and hoping by some magic it will become untangled isn't a helpful attitude – however understandable.

We also need another kind of courage. We need the courage to affirm our own potential for great achievement, our potential to change the world significantly. Maslow called our denial of this potential the *Jonah Complex*, and warned, "If you deliberately set out to be less than you are capable [of being], you'll be unhappy for the rest of your life."

Nisargadatta pointed out that there is a bit of faith needed to undertake an intuitive-stage practice. It's not the leap of faith that Christianity asked of us; it's the amount of faith required to repeat an experiment that some scientist has already run and reported on. "This is what I did, and this is what happened," the report says. You tentatively believe that. At least you believe it enough to repeat the experiment. You need that much faith.

Once under way, things begin to change for the better – slowly at times, with ups and downs – but unmistakably for the better. The mind gets quiet, and the first insights come. A budding confidence replaces the original apprehension – and from that point on enthusiasm builds, and a desire to continue.

In the final *experiential* stage, a radical change starts to take place. With the mind quiet, and the worst of the ego out of the way, the more profound knowledge, or Being, or Love – whatever we want to call it – starts to live the body/mind. It's as though this physical being is its avenue from the realm of potential into the realm of physical existence where it wants to express itself. It's as though it has been waiting with perfect patience for this body/mind to become willing to co-operate, to be taken over in a sense, to be lived by its values.

I first experienced this at a meditation retreat some years ago. Shortly before going on this retreat I had read *Freedom in Meditation*, an interesting book by Princeton psychologist Patricia Carrington. In it she told the story of a writer who had integrated meditation into the writing process. She said that he treated his "unconscious" mind like a "loyal servant." Before going to bed he would respectfully ask his unconscious to have the next material ready in the morning. Upon waking he would meditate for an hour, and then begin writing. The requested material would always be there.

When I read this I had no trouble believing that it worked, but I smiled at the loyal servant part. It seemed needlessly "personal." At one point during the retreat, however, I recalled the story and thought: Why not try it?

I had a problem at the time. I'd been struggling with a writing project, trying to find a good way of organizing the material, but with little success. I'd considered many approaches, but none seemed exactly right. So, I decided to respectfully ask my subconscious self to come up with an organization plan. Two hours later it did. The plan that popped into awareness was fresh, novel, and creative beyond my highest hopes. There was no way that "I" – the egoistic rational-mind me – could have done it.

Having that problem solved was wonderful, but having had the experience itself was even more important. From then on I had no doubt that the rational, verbal "I" shared this body with another intelligent presence. The feeling was uncanny, weird. This other presence, however, did not seem like a servant. It was at least an equal – or more likely, a superior. It behaved as though it had infinite patience, and was wiser than "I." But in another sense it was helpless. I realized that by itself it was totally isolated. On its own it couldn't talk and it couldn't act. It was as though it had always been there, just patiently waiting for the rational mind to quiet down and co-operate. It needed "me" as much as I needed it. And did I need it! The experience made me start thinking seriously about arranging my life so that the mental noise level would *stay* down. My rational mind was convinced that the two of us needed to work together.

In the experiential stage the body/mind is taking steps to insure that its activities are no longer directed by the old matrix of behaviour-determining drives and needs and fears. It actively wishes to be directed instead by this more profound intelligence. It wants to be only love – love in perception as interest and attention, and love in action as an agent through which the high values of Being become part of the informational world. The body-mind is still an energized, capable, decision-making node of process, but with a vast difference in inner peace and outer effectiveness.

One delightful part of all this is that the compulsion to be ceaselessly active fades away. The wisdom seems content to let the body/mind just *be* much of the time. When it's time to do, the body does – but it's effortless and natural – an organic integrated involvement with the larger process. The body is no longer run by reactive emotion and by the uptight rational mind that always before tried to control everything through serious plan-directed action.

It's almost as though when a mind/body allows itself to be lived by the Wisdom, the relaxation of *completion* settles down upon the event. The striving universe relaxes a bit. This little piece of process has come into harmony with its source.

Through a practice such as Vipassana, or Nisargadatta's meditation on the "I am" sense, or Da Free John's happiness practice, we eventually find a peaceful place where we can always go. Within that place mindstuff is just more stuff to watch pass by. The state is one of non-reactivity and quiet joy. It is the place one of my teachers called "home," and "a place of imperturbability." It is the "alone" space of Krishnamurti and the "loneliness" of Trungpa Rimpoche's Shambhala warrior. It is T.S. Eliot's "still point of the turning world." It is the still place of Being.

Staying in the quiet is the way you find and get familiar with that place. You are there whenever you see yourself as the still centre of witnessing awareness that is the real you. No matter if you-awareness get lost in the most horrendous fast-moving show; you can return to the place of stillness and watch that same show with compassionate detachment, unperturbed – once you know how. Finding this place and learning to return there is the key to liberation. Staying there is liberation. Again and again to return and say to yourself: "I am awareness watching the contents of consciousness." Awareness itself is the imperturbable space. And you are that awareness.

There are various ways of conceptualizing this end-process situation. The Theravadin Buddhist sees it as disidentification. The Universe (including human body/minds) is just impersonal process, and giving up the "wrong view" of identification with a body/mind liberates. The Vedantist sees it as a larger identification: Our true identity is the ground of the entire process. Making that switch of identity liberates. The Christian mystic sees an identity of Being: Our being and God's being are one. Experiencing that identity liberates. It is a single reality that these commentators are referring to, and their different concepts and verbal expressions highlight different aspects of that reality. All are legitimate ways of looking at it and describing it; all are partial and incomplete ways.

When you get a new perspective on something, when you come to see – with great depth and clarity – the illusion and distortion and limitation in your former view, then a permanent change takes place. After that you may occasionally forget to see things in the new way, but you can never really go back to the old mental space. You can't unsee what you've seen. You can't replace new clarity with old illusions.

In the liberated state there is freedom from domination by information – the body/mind's own brain-generated information. As I understand the Zen view of Nirvana, one "enters Nirvana" during those moments when there is a perfectly clear intuitive seeing-through of the curtain of information – during those moments when the mind is totally free of information's compulsive effects. Nirvana is always with us, always inherent in Samsara, yet ordinarily obscured by the mind's identification with the information that overlays or modulates Nirvana to produce Samsara. When that identification is finally and completely broken then awareness can watch with complete equanimity any informational show that the brain can create.[28]

Another way of looking at realization is this: There is an inherent dimension of depth to existence that we have been missing – a missing perspective that, when seen, makes everything stand out in three-dimensional bold relief. We could compare realization to the difference between viewing a slide in a slide viewer with its flat two-dimensional effect, and simultaneously viewing two slides taken from positions four inches apart. Seen through a stereo viewer (the old Viewmaster, or the like) the whole scene then springs into three-dimensional life. Realization adds the missing depth, the missing dimension of Being, to our view of the world. It provides us with intuitive cognizance of the cosmic medium to complement our sense-based perception of the cosmic message.

As radical transformation of the person takes place, what remains and what disappears? What can be expected as one nears the endpoint of the process? Combining what I see from my present vantage point in the early experiential stage with reports from others further along, I have formed a picture of life in the latter part of this stage. I'm sure that this picture will change somewhat as I continue my adventure in the years ahead; the reality will no doubt have its surprises. Nevertheless, it seems worthwhile to share this present view despite the risk that it might contain some errors of fact and emphasis.

As I see it the body, most mental and physical skills, voice, and appearance remain the same. But the reactivity is gone. Impulses of anger, hate, fear, jealousy, greed, craving and aversion arise at times. Sustained attention and energy are denied them, however, so they no longer become *states* of anger, hate, fear, etc. Positive mind states are present much more of the time: lovingkindness, patience, equanimity, compassion, joy at another's good fortune, etc. Old, limited, less correct models of reality are dropped, or are relegated to the special circumstances where they are appropriate. More holistic, more correct models are present much of the time.

These new models result in less judgement of others; there is a compassionate understanding that every body/mind is doing the best it can at every moment. What *is* at this moment must be. The mental/physical informational play that is unfolding at this instant is the inescapable effect of countless prior causes. It makes no sense to rail at present circumstances. What *is* at this moment simply *is*, the logical consequence of all that has gone before. Acceptance, therefore, is only rational, sane. Let me accept the present moment's inevitability and allow intuitive wisdom to guide this body/mind into the next. Let me accept an imperfect present so that I may transmute the next moment, and the next, into something just a little more loving, a little more harmonious, a little wiser. Let me observe the present moment with deep interest. Accept it. Then let it go.

Yes, these people have a profound acceptance of whatever is happening at this moment. They see this moment's frame of the informational show as a necessary unfolding of physical and mental causes. It might be possible to influence the next frame, but this one is spilled milk. Also, since these people live alertly, the intuitive process receives the information on current circumstances that it needs to guide them. Furthermore, their attentive observation turns off thought – keeping the mental noise down so that the inner guidance can be sensed.

Lastly, in these people the basic feeling of beingness, of identity, of dedication, has expanded outward, away from the body and from mind contents to include the whole universal process and its ground.

My impression is that once someone arrives at this mental way of living they almost always keep making the effort needed to stay there. I've heard a few stories about people far along the path who became alcoholics, or who got involved in sexual activities that caused suffering for others. I don't know if these stories are true or not – but I can see that they might be. The ancient brains are always going to be there – with their wanting, hating, survival-oriented programming still intact. They stay relatively quiet and benign when the right sort of mind habits are practised, but they are never conquered in any full or permanent sense. Ruth Benedict's work implies that each person has the potential to experience the full range of human mind states. Our particular life situation cultivates and reinforces certain mind-state potentials and fails to cultivate others. Spiritual practices are micro-cultures that change the cultivation and reinforcement balance – and as a result, the mind-state mix. Reversion to old negative patterns – or even the development of new ones – is still technically possible. What makes this unlikely to happen is not that the mind states attained are permanent, but that someone who reaches this point on the path sees with utter clarity the need to keep making the effort.

CHAPTER

11

Freedom

Wise people are said to be free, but just what does that mean? And what about will, choice, and responsibility?

Existentialist Hazel Barnes said: "Freedom is possibility." I agree. Yet there are different kinds and levels of possibility, and because of that, different kinds and levels of freedom.

There is what we could call intrinsic freedom, or ultimate freedom. I'm thinking here of wide-ranging possibility, possibility limited only by physical laws and available physical resources. I'm thinking of the things that could be done if enough human effort were focused on the task. World peace is an intrinsic possibility. So is freedom from hunger for all the world's people. And so is a quiet, alert mind. There is also what we could call psychologically-limited freedom. Here the range of possibility is much more limited – usually a tiny subset of the intrinsic possibilities.

I picture human freedom as a huge pasture. The pasture represents the full range of intrinsic possibility, the potential range of human freedom. The high fences that surround it are the fundamental, uncrossable limits of possibility. But individuals and societies don't have the run of the entire pasture. All live within much smaller corrals inside the big field. The corral fences are not prohibitively high. They can be climbed by individuals, and moved around by the concerted efforts of groups of people. While in place, however, they do limit individuals and social groups to much less than the run of the ranch. Many of these corral fences are mental fences, psychological fences. The limits they represent are the mental limits to freedom set by our attentiveness, by the values that run our frontal lobe's decision-making process, and by the information accessible at a given moment via perception and memory.

Freedom is possibility. In a similar vein Arthur Koestler said: "'Free will' is the awareness of alternate choices." I agree with this statement too – as far as it goes. Koestler's definition recognizes that we are unfree to the extent that we fail to understand what the intrinsic possibilities are; we are unfree to the extent that we are ignorant or deluded.

Yet there is more involved here than just information and perspective. Also involved are the internalized values that guide the choosing process. Many smokers are aware that not smoking is a possibility – a potential choice in some abstract, theoretical sense. Yet these people are not able to make that choice. Their present programming says: "Smoke!" And they do. The "free will" of these people is not free enough to allow them to say no to smoking. They see the range of options, but – at this moment – are not able to choose the non-smoking option.

Going back to our pasture metaphor, we could say that the mental corral fences come in two types. The first type is insufficient or misinterpreted information. Ignorance. Delusion. Not seeing the options. The second type is the fence of internalized values and goals – our programming. This fence can keep us from making certain choices even if the brain is aware of them as abstract possibilities.

The Existentialists, psychologist Benjamin Libet, and personal experience all agree: there is such a thing as conscious choice. Yet conscious choice is not free in the sense of being totally free from all influences. Decision making, like other forms of information processing, involves information inputs, value-based processing of that information, and information outputs (the products of that processing). Our actions at this moment are determined by the instructions our mental/physical executive process gives to the body at this moment. That decision is based on *something*– perhaps a thorough analysis, or a cursory analysis, or an intuitive hunch, or an ancient-brain impulse. If we are torn between two equal choices it might even be the "noise in the system" that tips the scale. But decisions don't come out of an informationless vacuum, they are based on, or caused by, some array of influences.

There is, therefore, an *instantaneous* determinism, a determinism of things as they are in this instant. You and I know, however, that things will not be the same in the next instant. We might perceive something we do not now perceive. We might get new information. Our brains might process the information we already have in some new way, and arrive at a new conclusion. We might have new insights into what is going on, and these insights might alter our internalized values.

Our default choosing system – at the bottom of the hierarchy of methods – is the automatic, reactive, ancient-brain choosing system that tends to get us into trouble. When that system is controlling, the hardwired survival values call the shots and determine our choices. Conscious choice, although not free from all influences, is a much more holistic choosing mechanism than reactive choice. It uplevels the choosing game.

Conscious choosing enters the picture at the level of intellect-based choice. The intellect can veto the various decisions-to-act made by that unconscious, reactive process – if our internalized values are ones that call for a veto, and if we are attentive enough. The values upon which decisions are made at this level include internalized cultural values, and values acquired or developed through personal experience.

At the third level, consciousness, intellect, and intuition all take part in the choosing process. Intuition appears to have access to more data than the intellect, and to "wise" values as well. In making intuition-based decisions, the intuitive process often takes subtle and peripheral data into account. It even seems to rank or weigh different factors according to their importance. The rational mind has trouble doing this. Have you ever tried to weigh, rationally, the pros and cons of two possible jobs, or moves, or relationships? Not only are there many factors to consider, but they all differ in relative importance. The intuitive process, however, somehow weighs everything and comes up with the needed decision. The process output at such times is often deceptively simple: just a yes or no feeling. GO or NOGO.

How do "wise" values become implanted in human beings? How is it that they are present to guide people in their best moments? There seem to be two possibilities. The first is that we pick them up from our culture along with many other values, and selectively sort them out of the mix as we gain life experience. The second is that we are born with wise values already embedded in our collective unconscious; they arise and start to run things if and when the ancient brains and the intellect quiet down and get out of the way.

Carl Jung was convinced that the intuitive process had access, not only to recallable memories and the contents of the personal unconscious, but also to the contents of a collective unconscious – to the full range of humanity's archetypes. Philip Goldberg wrote:

> To Jung, creativity and intuition implied a direct link between the conscious mind and deep archetypal structures. The archetypes have the power to confer meaningful interpretations to experience and to interject into a given situation their own impulses and thought formations. Intuitive people, said Jung, can perceive the inner processes and "supply certain data which may be of the utmost importance for understanding what is going on in the world." . . . In Jung's writings there are references to a variety of intuitive experiences, all attributed to the stirring of the collective unconscious.[29]

Maslow's theory holds that if we manage to meet our deficiency needs a new value will arise from subconscious realms and become a conscious motivator: *Become wise.* Once that value is firmly in place, something very special happens. We set off on a search to find out what this crazy game of existence is all about. We explore, and assimilate data. Then, one day, we find that our choices have become more intelligently determined. Why? Because the *seek wisdom* value is a master value that causes us to reassess our total array of values. With that value in place the corral fences that limit our freedom start moving back, and we begin to browse in that larger pasture. Our actions are determined by something, as always, but they are no longer determined as much by delusion and by drives such as greed and fear. They are determined instead by what *is,* by the situation, by reality, and by the values implicit in a holistic perspective. At that point, guided by what is real, and desirable for the whole, our actions

come into harmony with the larger process. We become free to choose the
sane way, the wise way, and the loving way, more of the time.

Those fortunate individuals who acquire this master value, and somehow manage to find support for their growth toward wisdom, discover
that in the far reaches of the process the uncomfortable, reactive, *need-to-
be-free* dissolves comfortably in commitment. They find a commitment
of effort that harmonizes their nature-as-a-person with the needs of
superordinate systems. The self-actualizing, self-transcending person has
gone beyond the need for that narcissistic I'll-do-what-I-want-when-I-
want-to sort of freedom. That has vanished with no regrets in the act of
appropriate commitment. These people have discovered something important: The most meaningful freedom in the universe (as well as the
most meaningful creativity) is connected with bringing the high values of
Being into actuality in the phenomenal world. Goethe put it this way:
"Freedom is nothing more than the opportunity to do what is reasonable
in all circumstances."

What about *responsibility?* Who is responsible for what? There are two
definitions of responsibility that interest us – and they sometimes get confused. There is responsibility in the sense of being able to choose right
rather than wrong. Moral responsibility. And there is responsibility in the
sense of being accountable. Let's first address the responsibility-for-choice
meaning.

Doesn't each person, at each moment, do what his or her brain/mind
decides is best at that moment? Each person's actions are the body's response
to a complex data-manipulating process involving internalized values, re-
membered information, programmed desires and aversions, and current
sensory input. The body acts in whatever way this total process decides that
it should act. Our seeing is limited, and a bunch of less than ideal evolution-
produced, family-produced, society-produced, circumstance-produced information and values end up determining what the action-decision will be.
Because of this, responsibility in the moral sense does not strike me as a
helpful concept. Given the process by which decisions are made, isn't everyone morally innocent? Isn't an attitude of forgiveness and compassion the
only rational attitude to have about human actions?

Obviously, people who are programmed to destroy cannot be allowed to run amok – but that is a different matter. **People are still responsible in the sense that they are accountable.** But we can stop being moralistic about it. It's just a question of what is best to do in a given set of circumstances: What course of action will maximize future harmony and minimize destruction?

The problem is not one of getting people to act more responsibly, it is one of helping them to see more deeply. For when they see, they will act "responsibly." For this to happen on a large scale we need a culture that encourages people to become wise, and supports them in that effort.

Seeing that we are not as free as we thought we were needn't depress us. Paradoxically, there is even something freeing about seeing the extent to which our choices are determined. For one thing, we can stop feeling guilty about not having enough willpower to realize our fantasies. We can replace the missing willpower with realistic, positive steps. We can put into place those kinds of reinforcing and motivating structures that will keep us moving toward our goals. The problem stops being an intangible will-o'-the-wisp thing. We no longer have to keep reaching for bootstraps of willpower that aren't there. All we have to do is arrange our lives so that we have enough exposure to positive influences – influences that promote and reinforce the kind of changes we are trying to make. Simple. And infinitely easier. There is no "I" who has to struggle. No impossible levels of self-discipline that must be maintained. The influences just do their work, and the earnest effort comes naturally.

Another plus is that compassion becomes simply rational. We see that **everyone is doing the best they can.**

Also, the way to uplevel the world process becomes clear: help create supportive environments and appropriate influences. Concentrate on basic needs, information, and motivation. People whose basic needs are met, and who are exposed to the right influences at the right times in their lives, will be motivated to become "good" people.

CHAPTER

12

Wiser Relating

Were I an expert in interpersonal relationships I might devote several chapters to wise relating, but I am not one, either by training or natural gift. I, like many other men, have been a slow learner in this area. Still, I can't totally bypass this important topic, and a few hard-won perspectives seem worth mentioning.

One bit of clarity concerns the role of relationships as an indicator of how well we are doing. There are some highly loving, nurturing, non-reactive people who, to become wiser, need to go after additional conceptual knowledge. They need to further develop their intellectual side. For the rest of us, however – for men in general, and particularly men like me who have been steeped in rationality – the main challenges are to transcend reactivity and broaden our sense of identity. For us, our relationships with other people provide the most reliable moment-to-moment test of how well we are progressing toward wisdom. Keeping this in mind helps us avoid mistaking means for ends. People who are trying to become wiser sometimes get so caught up in the techniques, trappings, and paraphernalia of the path that they forget the goal. The ultimate test of our progress is not how long or how often we meditate, it is whether we act non-reactively toward others; it is whether we treat them with love, compassion, and deep understanding in all our encounters with them.

Our intimate relationships are where we put what we've learned about freedom and commitment to the most severe test. My early intimate relationships were rooted in sexual attraction, in avoiding the pain of loneliness, and in the desire for relational peace and security – the desire to have this other person, on tap, permanently, to provide a warm secure background to my life. It was an immature (if all too typical) way of relating. Later, after I became interested in my own inner development, I ran across some words of Ranier Maria Rilke which pointed to a very different relationship ideal:

> ... the love that consists in this, that two solitudes protect and border and salute each other.

That was more like it. Yet I found it both difficult and painful to move from an intellectual resonance with that thought to living it all day, every day. Eventually the truth began to dawn; a truly healthy primary relationship was only possible if I transcended my own neediness. At that point I needed. And I needed to be needed. Was it possible to let go of the need-meeting aspect of an intimate relationship? Was it possible to be satisfied with what the other was willing to offer at any given moment? Was it possible to move from needing, seeking, clinging, and fear-of-loss to truly loving, to continuous well-wishing, to continuous respect and support for the other's chosen quest? I didn't know, but I spent much time during those years struggling to find out.

As you know, the meditation retreats I attended profoundly changed my perspective on the world; they also changed my perspective on relationships. During a three-month retreat in 1984 I had some insights that addressed the commitment issue. To wiser people they might simply represent common sense, but I'll pass them along for consideration by other slow learners.

The insights that arose addressed the issue of commitment in a primary relationship. The first thing that struck home was that commitment meant having long-run intentions about the relationship – an open-ended attitude toward it, no anticipated end to it. I also saw that deep intimacy requires deep trust, and for that level of trust to develop one needed to be sexually faithful. I realized that even a secret one-time epi-

sode – one which the other might never know about – would have a rela-
tionship-damaging effect in my own mind. It was simple. If you were
committed, you were committed. You remained worthy of trust.

Commitment also meant not abandoning the relationship – at least
for awhile – if the other breached trust or decided to end the relationship.
Standing by after the apparent end for perhaps a year without getting intimately involved with anyone else made sense. If the relationship had
been worth open-ended commitment in the past, it was worth this pause
to make sure it was truly over. People do change their minds, after all, and
the apparently irresolvable sometimes works itself out.

Regarding more mundane relationship problems, it seemed that commitment meant searching creatively for all-win answers. It meant not accepting the surface assumption that if one person wins the other must
lose. It meant hunting for some approach which enhances the whole situation – searching for that un-thought-of opportunity, that forgotten aspect of the situation that could be turned into a plus for both.

Lastly, it meant the intent to share – deeply and fully – the content of
my mind with the other. Share my thoughts and feelings without decep-
tion. I would tell no overt lies, of course. And no intentional lies-of-omis-
sion, no "willed areas of opacity" as Existentialist Hazel Barnes put it.
Since we humans are vulnerable and fearful beings, it was also clear that
trust-building and barrier-removing are gradual processes. Making it to
the deepest levels of intimacy takes time.

Some months later the Rilkean ideal of a relationship between two
solitudes moved down from the intellect to became part of my deeper
understanding. As a person I was alone, yet in Reality I was totally connected with everything. It was the *feelings* of aloneness and loneliness that
were the troublemakers – feelings generated by those ancient parts of my
brain. The important thing was to tolerate – no, to accept fully – those
feelings whenever they arose. Immersion in togetherness (to use that
once-popular 1950s term) in an effort to make those feelings go away was
not an appropriate way of dealing with them. Only by accepting them
was it possible to have a mature intimate relationship. The need for personal independence also became crystal clear. Each intelligent node of

process needs to run its own show, to try its own experiments. Control, in all its subtle and not-so-subtle forms, was inappropriate.

When I fully accepted these conditions, then Rilke's words about two solitudes protecting, bordering, and saluting each other were no longer just words. They became a comfortable and appropriate way of seeing and living relationship.

I'm reminded of a story about Gurdjieff and food. I assume that this spiritual teacher was not driven by compulsive desires for food. He nevertheless enjoyed and appreciated it, and was said to keep many delicacies around. He was beyond craving food, but enjoyed it aesthetically. Similarly, when we stop craving the elimination of lonely feelings, when we lose our compulsive need to get rid of them, it then becomes possible for a new level of appreciation to open up – an aesthetic sort of enjoyment. When we no longer need the other as an instrument to meet our needs, we then become free to appreciate that person as they are, for what they are – and to delight in that.

My understanding of how important it is for each partner to have a rich, full, satisfying life outside the relationship also deepened. The metaphor of intimate relationship as dessert came to mind. Dessert is a pleasant addition to a meal, but not a satisfactory substitute for the main course. If we expect our primary relationship to meet all our needs, we're in trouble. We can't live on dessert alone; to try is to put an impossible burden on the relationship. We must involve ourselves with life outside the relationship in ways that help us meet our esteem and self-actualization needs.

CHAPTER

13

A Wisdom-Based Culture

Despite some hints of progress, particularly in Holland and Scandinavia, our present industrial cultures are far from being wisdom-based cultures. They actively support the early stages of growth but not the later ones. Thus, to become wise in our present culture we must either be very lucky, very resourceful, or both. In general, we must find supportive subcultures, or create around ourselves supportive micro-cultures. This do-it-yourself approach will work for truly dedicated individuals, but it's not apt to create the large numbers of wise people needed to make mind-directed evolution a success. For that to happen, mainstream cultures must change.

Is there any hope of transforming our present society into one that would produce many such people? I see some encouraging signs. For one thing, there are growing numbers of people who pursue wisdom-fostering practices without society's help. They are right now creating networks, support groups, and institutions that are prototypes of the structures needed in a wisdom-centred society. Also encouraging are the signs of readiness on a larger scale. Some positive pre-conditions already exist in the cultures of the industrial nations. These readiness factors are analogous to soil, water, and fertilizer. If more of the right seeds are now planted, many more people will adopt *becoming wise* as a consciously held value and pursue that adventure. These factors are:

Leisure. Most of us have time that could be devoted to the pursuit of wisdom. In U.S. households with TV sets, the average adult watches more than 4.5 hours of TV per day. Employment patterns are changing too. More people are sharing jobs, taking leaves of absence or sabbaticals, and just plain quitting work for periods of time. Others – the unemployed – have enforced leisure, but leisure nonetheless. It could be used for growth. By legitimizing time off for growth-fostering, wisdom-fostering pursuits, governments could reduce pressure from the public to create more jobs.

The cultural stress on delayed satisfaction. Perhaps it is less prevalent in the generations younger than mine. Still, most of us in the industrial world have some experience working hard now for rewards later.

Cheap books and transportation. Unlike 50 years ago, there is today relatively easy access to spiritual teachers and teachings. The word is getting out.

The motivating influence of the wise, and those involved in becoming wise. Their numbers increase all the time, and so their influence increases. (The very few once motivated the few who now motivate the more . . .)

Affluence. Many people in the industrial countries have the money needed to buy books, attend retreats, etc., if this becomes one of their priorities.

For the first time in history, many people "have it good" in a material and psychological sense. Their struggle for material comfort, security, and even status has been won. They now face the question: "What next?" "What will be the source of meaning in my life?" Many of these people are choosing to take the inner journey toward wisdom despite the present difficulties. In earlier eras, before material sufficiency, grasping for pleasure was necessary and appropriate. It had survival value for the species. Now, faced with a gentler situation, many are starting to explore the option of not grasping for pleasure, and are finding a deeper, quieter, richer, happier place – a place to Be. Later, with their new perspectives, these people will help society as a whole become more supportive for the inner journeys of their children and grandchildren.

Wisdom is not one monolithic way of being that eliminates all differences between people; wisdom takes many different forms. Futurist Barbara Marx Hubbard has said that a whole "ecology of souls" will be needed to create and populate this new, wiser culture. What varieties of wisdom do you see as important? Here is my list:

- To help world society deal with its complex problems we need Phase 2 evolutionaries – people having well-developed intellects and worldly skills who have taken that extra giant-step and have freed themselves, to a large extent, from the tyranny of the wanting/ condemning mind.

- We need those people who are led to spend their whole lives in spiritual practice. We need them as researchers for better ways. We need them as teachers and guides in tomorrow's schools of wisdom. We need them to show us, through the examples of their lives, what life is like at the far reaches of the path.

- We need people who have led full rich lives and have grown in wisdom to function as *life management counsellors.* They are needed to help others deal with the existential crises in their lives. To help them find meaning. To help them discover what they really want to do. To help them lay realistic plans for doing it. And to discuss wisdom and the process of spiritual development.

- We need people in ordinary life roles who are earnest about becoming wise and are making progress at that. We need the wisdom they bring to all their daily activities.

Becoming wise is what matters, personally and globally. Growth of wisdom in social action and livelihood. Growth of wisdom in relationships. Growth in understanding of what it's all about. There is the path of knowledge and the path of wisdom. Highly motivated people attend university and perhaps graduate school – seeking knowledge and the other benefits of a degree. Now, highly motivated people are starting to seek wisdom – another difficult undertaking. There are no absolute assurances when one begins either endeavor, and there are dropouts from both. But for those who go a reasonable distance down either path there are significant payoffs.

The task is to become wise – despite present difficulties – and try to build a culture in which wisdom will not only be possible but will be the norm, *normal.* The world is what it is. Considering everything that has gone before, it couldn't, today, be any different. So there is no point regretting or recriminating. But there is a lot of point in making the next moment better – and the next and the next. Our culture may be slow to change, but our culture is not our enemy. Our culture is, in fact, a direct reflection of *us* – or at least the us of yesterday. We must help our culture grow and mature, help it mirror the wisdom-seeking us of today and tomorrow.

I have no illusion that total global transformation will happen overnight. The industrial nations might undergo a significant degree of transformation within a generation or two, but it is not likely to happen globally until the basic needs of all the world's people are met – not just physical needs, but all of Maslow's deficiency needs.

Meanwhile, we will still need political action. Material sufficiency must reach everyone. The ecological, population, and nuclear time bombs must be defused, and there are other pressing problems. Unfortunately, political action does nothing to correct the deeply-rooted underlying problem. Again and again humanity has had to face war and violence and the results of greed because it has not dealt effectively with the mental roots of those behaviours. Corrective environmental action and nuclear disarmament would buy us time for the needed psychological/cultural transformation, but unless humanity becomes wiser, the same problems will someday be back. Many short term actions are important – vital in fact. But **whatever short term actions we take, we also need to be working on the long term psyche-based solution.** Taking steps now to become wise is not another elitist retreat from the problems experienced by the majority of the world's people. It is, in fact, the most effective possible long-term attack on those problems.

People in many countries are today in the position of those Scottish Highlanders three hundred years ago: neglected, exploited, and struggling desperately to survive. What is more, too often we in the North are like the King's man, the Earl of Argyll, just making things worse. Third World people often say to would-be do-gooders from the industrial world, "Go home. Work there. Help get your nation's boot off our necks." They tell us that they don't need us to do good for them nearly as much as they need us to stop doing bad to them. At the moment, many industrial nations are guilty of Band-Aid do-gooding atop crass exploitation and pervasive unconcern. As societies, we have not yet become wise enough to take the boot off their necks.

This situation must change. And it *will* change. The rampant narcissism and greed of our age will end. It will end, either in upward transformation, or in the classic disintegration typical of past empires. We will become either a wisdom-based society, a footnote in the history books of some future culture, or worse yet, a totally forgotten failed experiment on a dead planet.

Joseph Campbell outlined our task in these words:

The modern hero-deed must be that of questing to bring to light again the lost Atlantis of the co-ordinated soul. Obviously, this work cannot be wrought by turning back, or away, from what has been accomplished by the modern revolution; for the problem is nothing if not that of rendering the modern world spiritually significant – or rather (phrasing the same principle the other way round) nothing if not that of making it possible for men and women to come to full human maturity through the conditions of contemporary life. . . . The modern hero, the modern individual who dares to heed the call and seek the mansion of that presence with whom it is our whole destiny to be atoned, cannot, indeed must not, wait for his community to cast off its slough of pride, fear, rationalized avarice, and sanctified misunderstanding. "Live," Nietzsche says, "as though the day were here." It is not society that is to guide and save the creative hero, but precisely the reverse.[30]

As compassion arises in the latter stages of the process, as holistic seeing makes the outrageous behaviour of our cultural institutions clearer, as people become more sensitive to situations where they have some leverage, the intuitive wisdom will guide them into various forms of wise, effective action. I have no doubt about this. There is a time to detach, and a time to engage. In the coming years there will be the opportunity – and the necessity – for both. We can't afford to neglect either, and I don't think we will.

I see rapid progress toward a wisdom-based culture once the present consensus view of reality starts to be replaced by a new one – particularly when the personal-identity perspective begins to be replaced on a large scale by the unitive view. History shows us that even the most well-entrenched erroneous views can be dropped rapidly when enough influential people get a new, more valid perspective on the same old data. For eons it was perfectly clear to everyone that the earth stood still and the sun, moon and stars revolved around the earth. The sun rose every morning in the east, travelled across the sky, and set every evening in the west. Simple, and totally obvious. Yet Copernicus, in 1543, turned all that around by saying no, we had it wrong, the earth rotates, and it travels around the sun. Communication wasn't all that great in those days, and science itself was not a massive enterprise, but when Kepler and Newton adopted the Copernican ideas and started to build on them a century later, the old delusion quickly faded away.

More recent revolutions in perspective have happened even more quickly. The assumption that the earth was formed a few thousand years ago held sway until James Hutton in 1780 and Charles Lyell in 1830 established the geologic "deep time" perspective. This in turn laid the foundation for Charles Darwin, a few decades after that, to overturn the prevailing assumption that a master-designer God had created all nature's marvels and put them on earth all at one time. In our own century the process has accelerated even more. The revolution in perspective from Newtonian to relativistic physics happened within two or three decades.

Copernican ideas did – and still do – go against perceptual common sense. It *feels* as though the earth is standing still, and we *see* the sun move across the sky. Yet no one today doubts the truth of the Copernican insights. We still talk about the sun rising and setting, but we all know that it's just a way of speaking. If anything conflicts with that view we immediately flip to the true one. I think the day will come when we will do that with the person-centred perspective. We will talk about being persons for convenience, as we talk about the sun rising and setting. But we will never for a moment be fooled into believing that this personal identity is our deep, true identity. From the time children are little they will know that they have two identities – a temporary information-based identity as a person, and a permanent identity as Being. Effective techniques will be worked out to help them realize this permanent identity intuitively and experientially as well as intellectually.

If humanity doesn't self-destruct in the meantime, I'm sure that people 200 years from now will slowly shake their heads and smile at the superstitions, the primitive rituals, and the ignorant perspectives of people back in the twentieth century. I can hear it now: "Did you know that for much of that century science actually denied the existence of mentality?" "Did you know that their primitive culture had an institution called advertising that did everything in its power to inflame people's desires – actually *inflame* them rather than quiet them?" "Did you know that they watched the portrayal of violent acts on coloured screens for *entertainment*?" "Did you know that they associated the universal sense of identity with only their bodies and mind contents, and not with Being?"

Some of this stuff is already beginning to seem crazy to large numbers of people. I suspect that one of these decades an avalanche effect will occur, and some important shifts in perspective will happen rapidly, on a mass scale. I even heard one reasoned guess about which decade. Near the end of that three-month retreat, a Korean Zen Master spoke to us. Someone asked him about the future of the world, and about combining social action with spiritual practice. In his reply the Zen Master noted that in the late '60s there was a humanistic, anti-violence feeling among young people all over the world – not just in Western industrial countries, but in communist countries and the Third World too. He was confident that when the people of this "Woodstock Generation" reach their 50s and assume positions of power – about the year 2000 – the world will take a significant turn for the better.

That generation has been called a generation of innocent idealists. Most have lost their innocence by now, and many have taken sidetracks and detours – but I suspect that the core of idealism is still there. Perhaps that Zen Master is right. The decade between 2000 and 2010 just might be a time of inflection in the history of the world – one of those historic moments when intelligent effort really does produce large-scale change. Just maybe the people of the world will get together then and make real progress in moving the corral fences back toward the ultimate limits of possibility.

For such a turning point to arise the wisdom must exist, and for that to happen much inner preparing must take place between now and then. I can't think of a more significant focus for my own life during the 1990s. How about you?

C H A P T E R

14

References and Resources

If you are intrigued by some of the ideas, perspectives, or practices presented in the preceding chapters, you might want to browse through this final one. I comment briefly on certain books that I have found especially helpful, and give the names and addresses of some meditation centres, teachers, and sitting groups.

The Outward-Oriented Adventure

It is clear to me now that the decade of my 30s was a period of development and preparation, a period in which I tried dreams on for fit, lived a few to their natural ends, and a few others until it seemed time to drop them. If I lived this decade again, its details would be different, but I hope not its spirit. Living your 20s and 30s intensely, with your own growth consciously in mind, is not the worst possible preparation for those more contemplative decades that come later.

I owe much to several of the people I met early in this period. They were people who lived in a realm of ideas. They saw what was going on in the world at a superficial level, as I did – but they saw more. They were able to connect the surface facts with an array of concepts and models and perspectives residing at some deeper level. I realized that to gain access to this other level you had to read – read selectively because there wasn't enough time to read everything, but read a lot.

My friends suggested several possible starting points, one of these being French Existentialism. I read Sartre's *Being and Nothingness* and his *Existentialism and Human Emotions*. Parts of the first book were beyond me, but I was drawn to Sartre's basic thesis: Human nature is not a determinism set up in advance by God or Nature. Instead, human nature is defined moment-to-moment by how we human beings actually live our lives – by the lifelong string of choices each of us makes. Sartre stressed that how we act in the world is what counts, not our good intentions. Each life is nothing more nor less than the sum of the actions that comprise it. Personal immortality resides only in the effect which those actions have on the world. Since we are condemned to choose, we might as well make our choices with as much awareness as possible. It makes sense to choose consciously what we want to do with our lives, and to move toward the chosen goal.

Camus's theme was similar to Sartre's but had its individual slant. I especially liked Camus's personal journals: *Notebooks 1935-1942* and *Notebooks 1942-1951*. Camus stressed the need to create meaning in the universe through artistic creativity and love – love not just in the romantic sense, but also love as deep friendship and lovingkindness. He realized that art was commentary on life, and felt that the great artist must first have a "great experience of life." Furthermore, love would play a central role in this "great experience."

Love is the main theme of Lawrence Durrell's "Alexandria Quartet." Reading the four interlinked volumes in the intended order – *Justine, Balthazar, Mountolive,* then *Clea* – leads the reader through a progression of love's many forms and guises – both immature and highly mature ones.

Nikos Kazantzakis was another writer who inspired and motivated me. *Zorba the Greek* was a call to adventure that I found compelling. I lived from my head. Zorba lived from his guts. He was totally engaged in the present moment, and always saw the world with fresh eyes. He lived each moment fully – right to the bursting point. He was inner-directed to the extreme, and seemed to be beyond fear. He was always willing to risk – to risk everything. No wonder Kazantzakis was fascinated with Zorba, and drawn to his mode of living. I was too.

Kazantzakis told the story of his own struggle to become wise in *Report to Greco.* In it he related many adventures – including an account of his relationship with the real-life Zorba. Interwoven with the narrative was the Kazantzakis philosophy of life – and it was this that I found both powerful and personally relevant. Kazantzakis chose one word to characterize his life: *ascent.* Always he had kept his eye on the farthest limit; always he had tried to attain the greatest height. His central message was this: Find that significant task or battle for which you are best suited, then pour your energy into it. Perceive. Love. Live the totality.

Theories of Psychological-Spiritual Growth

Abraham Maslow

Maslow's books are tremendously rich. They have many levels of meaning and message, and at each reading you hear what you are ready to hear. Four of them make my recommended list. The oldest is *Motivation and Personality.* First published in 1954, it summarizes Maslow's work to that point; it outlines his theory of motivation and his research into the characteristics of self-actualizing people. In *Toward a Psychology of Being* Maslow gets into the connections between Humanistic Psychology and Existentialism. He expands and clarifies his theory of motivation. And he discusses peak experiences. His posthumous book, *The Farther Reaches of Human Nature* deals with "Cosmic" self-actualization and self-transcendence – the spiritual end-process of personal growth. In it he also discusses some interesting aspects of Anthropologist Ruth Benedict's work. The fourth book, *Religions, Values, and Peak Experiences* deals with intrinsic values and with varieties of spiritual experience.

Ken Wilber

Wilber showed me that mental development is a vast spectrum on which the Freudians, Behaviourists, and various spiritual disciplines all have legitimate places. He makes it clear that seeming contradictions – like using one form of therapy to build an ego and another to tear it down – make sense if the right thing is done at the right stage of our inner development. It's not all intellectual, either. His reports on the far reaches of the spectrum have the aura of first hand reports. My favourite of his books is *No Boundary: Eastern and Western Approaches to Personal Growth*. Another, which goes into the spectrum concept in more detail, is *The Spectrum of Consciousness*. A third, which deals with evolution and mind is *Up From Eden: A Transpersonal View of Human Evolution*.

The Perennial Philosophy
(Practices that involve reidentification with Being.)

Buddhist writings

There are several writings from Buddhism's Zen tradition that express the perennial philosophy with clarity and impact. Two of my favourites are "The Lankavatara Sutra," and the discourse by the Third Patriarch of Zen on "Believing in Mind." These, the famous "Oxherding Pictures of Zen," and much other worthwhile material appears in *The Manual of Zen Buddhism* by the late Zen scholar D. T. Suzuki.

The Cloud of Unknowing

Written by an anonymous Christian mystic in the 14th Century, *The Cloud of Unknowing* now appears in an edition with a more mature work by the same author: *The Book of Privy Counseling*. The first book links contemplative practice with traditional Christianity. The second focuses on the essence of the practice itself. I especially like the second.

Da Free John

Although initially put off by Da Free John's guru-with-ardent-followers image, I came to agree with Ken Wilber that Free John was saying important things, and saying them clearly. In *Nirvanasara* Free John presents the perennial philosophy as he sees it: an integration of Advaita Vedanta (the view held by Vedantists like Nisargadatta), and Buddhism. *The Bodily Location of Happiness* focuses on Free John's "Happiness" practice. His autobiography, *The Knee of Listening* (published under his original name, Franklin Jones), also sheds light on this practice.

Aldous Huxley

Huxley was a Western intellectual with a Christian background who discovered the wisdom of the East – and also discovered that this wisdom is identical with the wisdom spoken of by the Christian mystics of the Middle Ages. In *The Perennial Philosophy*, he shares some of the teachings of Eastern and Western mysticism, and adds his own lucid and informed commentary.

Lao Tzu

Two works are attributed to Taoist sage Lao Tzu: the well-known *Tao Te Ching*, and a compilation of later teachings called the *Hua Hu Ching*. Both are available in a volume entitled *The Complete Works of Lao Tzu*. The first presents the Taoist view of what *is*, the second deals with the Taoist form of perennial philosophy practice. Many translations of the *Tao Te Ching* are available; my favourite is the recent Stephen Mitchell translation that uses contemporary language and imagery.

Nisargadatta

If I could take only a few books with me to a desert island, *I Am That: Conversations With Sri Nisargadatta Maharaj* would be one of them. Nisargadatta, you may have discovered in the chapter notes, was a former Bombay cigarette maker who made a permanent gestalt flip of re-identification. Separated from the author of *The Book of Privy Counseling* by culture, distance, and 600 years, these two nevertheless watched the world from the same mental space. And they advocated the same practice to reach that space: pay attention as continuously as possible to the elemental sense of being, of existing.

Alan Watts

The Book: On the Taboo Against Knowing Who You Are is Alan Watts's lucid discussion of the unitive view, and of the difficulty we have in seeing things that way. In an earlier work, *The Meaning of Happiness: The Quest for Freedom of the Spirit in Modern Psychology and the Wisdom of the East* he presents his views about happiness.

Joseph Campbell

I didn't discover Joseph Campbell until he became popular in the 1980s – what a pity! In *Hero With a Thousand Faces* Campbell contends that the great mythic hero stories of cultures all over the world symbolize the universal search for wisdom and Self-realization, the universal struggle to make the perennial philosophy our own.

Mindfulness Meditation (Vipassana)

Joseph Goldstein and Jack Kornfield

Joseph Goldstein is one of the founders of the Insight Meditation Society; Jack Kornfield has taught Vipassana there (and elsewhere) for many years. Their book, *Seeking the Heart of Wisdom: The Path of Insight Meditation,* is the fruit of their many years of teaching experience. It goes into the "why" of mindfulness practice, and relates it to other Buddhist teachings. *The Experience of Insight: A Simple and Direct Guide to Buddhist Meditation* is an earlier book on the practice by Joseph Goldstein. It, too, is worthwhile.

Thich Nhat Hanh

Thich Nhat Hanh is the Vietnamese Zen Master who headed the Vietnamese Buddhist Peace Delegation in Paris during the Vietnam War. He has written two wonderful books on the practice of mindfulness meditation: *The Miracle of Mindfulness,* and *Peace is Every Step.*

Stephen Levine

Stephen Levine's book, *A Gradual Awakening,* describes the changes in outlook and understanding that take place as mindfulness practice continues and deepens. It is another of my "desert island" books – one that leads me to deeper understanding on each re-reading. I find it the perfect complement to a mindfulness meditation practice.

Information on retreats led by Stephen Levine, and cassette recordings of his talks and guided meditations, are available from The Hanuman Foundation Tape Library, Box 61498, Santa Cruz, CA 95061. The Foundation also distributes Ram Dass tapes.

Sitting Groups

It is helpful to have friends with whom to share the practice, and Vipassana sitting groups have sprung up in many North American cities. Some Canadian contacts are:

Calgary, Alberta
Calgary Theravadin Meditation Group
c/o Shirley Johannesen
3212-6th St. S.W.
Calgary, Alberta T2S 2M3
(403) 243-3433

Courtenay, British Columbia
Susan Brooks (604) 338-6253

Vancouver, British Columbia
Karuna Meditation Society
#19-555 West 12th Avenue
Vancouver, B.C. V5Z 4L6
Richard Piers (604) 222-4941

Winnipeg, Manitoba
Keith Millan (206) 237-8866

Hamilton, Ontario
(416) 525-2865

Lindsay, Ontario
Norman Feldman (705) 878-0829

Ottawa, Ontario
(613) 235-2725 or (613) 563-1697

Toronto, Ontario
Toronto Vipassana Community
666 Balliol Street
Toronto, Ontario M4S 1E7
(416) 488-5485

Paul MacRae
14 Cluny Drive

Toronto, Ontario M4W 2P7
(416) 924-5574

Nine Mountain Zen Gate
8-1268 King Street West
Toronto, Ontario M6K 1G5
(416) 534-6935

Charlottetown, Prince Edward Island
The U.P.E.I. Meditation Group
John DeGrace (902) 566-0439 or (902) 569-3868

For information on sitting groups in U.S. cities contact The Insight Meditation Society, Pleasant St., Barre, Massachusetts 01005. Phone (508) 355-4378.

Meditation Retreats and Tapes

Information on Vipassana retreats held at the Insight Meditation Center in Barre, Massachusetts and other parts of the world is available from The Insight Meditation Society (IMS), Pleasant Street, Barre, MA 01005 (508) 355-4378. Many weekend and nine-day retreats are held each year at the Center, as well as a three-month retreat traditionally held each fall from mid-September to mid-December. Cassette recordings of evening talks made during IMS retreats are available through the Dharma Seed Tape Library, 1041 Federal Street, Belchertown, MA 01007.

IMS has now expanded to the West Coast. Insight Meditation West holds retreats at Spirit Rock Center located in Marin County north of San Francisco. Their address is P.O. Box 909, 5000 Sir Francis Drake Blvd., Woodacre, CA 94973. (415) 488-0164. They also have a recorded message line: (415) 488-0170.

Vipassana retreats are held in British Columbia, Canada under the auspices of the Karuna Meditation Society, #19-555 West 12th Avenue, Vancouver, B.C. V5Z 4L6, Phone: Richard Piers (604) 222-4941

S.N. Goenka is a Vipassana teacher from India who moved to the U.S. and established The Vipassana Meditation Center, P.O. Box 24, Shelburne Falls, MA 01370 (413) 625-2160.

There are two Vipassana retreat centres in England. One is Gaia House, Denbury, near Newton Abbot, Devon TQ12 5HU England Phone: Ipplepen (0803) 813188. The second is Amaravati Buddhist Centre, Great Gaddesden, Hemel Hempstead, Herefordshire, HP1 3BZ England Phone: International code 44-44284-2455.

The Cambridge Insight Meditation Centre

Larry Rosenberg is a Vipassana teacher whose special focus is helping city people deepen their practice and integrate mindfulness into their daily lives. He leads several retreats each year at IMS in Barre, but spends most of his time at the Cambridge Insight Meditation Center (CIMC) which he founded in 1985. The Center, housed in a three-story Victorian house, provides a quiet refuge from the hustle-bustle of Boston/Cambridge. CIMC provides opportunities for daily sitting, weekend retreats, weekly talks by local and visiting teachers, and of course, Larry. I can't imagine a more supportive environment for the urban student; let's hope the idea spreads. For information on the Center's services and programmes, write to CIMC, 331 Broadway, Cambridge, MA 02139 or call (617) 491-5070.

Some Other Perspectives

William James

The turn-of-the-century psychologist William James took a perceptive look at mystical experience in *The Varieties of Religious Experience*. James, too, believed in looking directly at what was happening in the mind – an approach that went out of psychological fashion a few years later.

Kazantzakis

One slant on people as agents of evolution was given by Nikos Kazantzakis in his poetic book, *The Saviors of God*. Kazantzakis saw evolution as a bloody war of ascent from chaos to high possibility being waged by a less than almighty God – a God that needs help from human beings and all other creatures.

Krishnamurti

I left Krishnamurti out of the Perennial Philosophy section because he avoided cosmological speculation and talk about reidentification – focusing instead on exploring moment to moment mental happenings. My favourite among his many books is *The First and Last Freedom* which I find particularly clear and complete. I also like the three volume *Commentaries on Living* series. His descriptions of the world around him in these latter books are priceless glimpses into his mind – the mind of a man who lived each moment with intense alertness and sensitivity.

Open Focus

The Open Focus Handbook and *Open Focus* cassettes are available from Biofeedback Computers, Inc., P.O. Box 572, Princeton, NJ 08540.

Chogyam Trungpa

The late Chogyam Trungpa, Rimpoche was a Tibetan Buddhist teacher who fled Tibet at the time of the Chinese takeover in 1959. He was educated at Oxford in the '60s, founded Naropa Institute in Boulder, Colourado in the '70s, and started the Naropa Institute of Canada in Halifax, Nova Scotia in the 1980s. He also wrote several helpful books. In *Cutting Through Spiritual Materialism* he pointed out some spiritual traps into which we North Americans frequently fall – ways that we use spiritual practices to strengthen ego rather than destroy it. A more recent book, *Shambhala: The Sacred Path of the Warrior* also focused on trouble spots, on those difficult and painful places on the path that we can't bypass if we are serious about growing.

Other Personal Growth Resources

I mentioned *A Life of One's Own* by Joanna Field. A comprehensive and recent overview of intuition is *The Intuitive Edge: Understanding Intuition and Applying It in Everyday Life* by Philip Goldberg. A more scholarly book on intuition, but one rich in detail is Tony Bastick's *Intuition: How We Think and Act*. Roberto Assagioli's *Psychosynthesis* presents the details of his multifaceted therapy. Another book I found helpful was *Transitions:*

Making Sense of Life's Changes by William Bridges. Bridges, by naming and talking about that fuzzy, uncomfortable stage between endings and new beginnings, legitimizes it. He also deals with helpful, and not so helpful, ways of going through these transitions.

The Scientific Big Picture

Cosmology

Stephen Weinberg's *The First Three Minutes: A Modern View of the Origin of the Universe* presents the currently accepted model of the origin of the universe. *The Scientific American* does an excellent job of updating this picture every year or two with the latest theories, and the latest developments in cosmology and particle physics. Stephen Hawking's *A Brief History of Time* is worth reading, as are *In Search of the Big Bang* by John Gribbin and *The Cosmic Blueprint* by Paul Davies.

Evolution

For a variety of perspectives you might read Ervin Laszlo's *Evolution: The Grand Synthesis*, Richard Dawkins's *The Blind Watchmaker*, and at least one of Stephen Jay Gould's books (*Time's Arrow, Time's Cycle*, for example).

Brain/Mind

Paul MacLean (*A Triune Concept of Brain and Behavior*) and Melvin Konner (*The Tangled Wing*) do a good job of presenting the biological basis for reactive emotion and behaviour. See the Chapter 6 **Notes** for references to Benjamin Libet's work on the relationship between consciousness and intention. Arguments for mind being separate from matter are presented by Eccles and Robinson in *The Wonder of Being Human*. The view that mind and matter are two aspects of a single underlying reality is made by Gordon Globus, Bernard Rensch, and Ervin Laszlo – see their listings in the Chapter 1 **Notes**. Refer to the Roger Sperry articles listed in the Chapter 6 **Notes** for his view that mind is a system-emergent of the brain that can have a top-down influence back on brain functioning.

Models, Metaphors, and Information
An excellent book on the nature of information and its many roles is
Jeremy Campbell's *Grammatical Man: Information, Entropy, Language,
and Life.* My understanding of natural systems owes much to the writing
of Ervin Laszlo, a former concert pianist with a doctorate from the
Sorbonne who became an expert on systems and the author of several
Club of Rome studies. His book, *The Systems View of the World,* is a book
for the general reader that looks at nature and human beings from the
system point of view. A more scholarly work is Laszlo's *Introduction to
Systems Philosophy: Toward a New Paradigm of Contemporary Thought.*

Notes

Chapter 1 – What Is Wisdom?

1. Abraham Maslow, *Toward a Psychology of Being*, Second Edition, New York: Van Nostrand Reinhold, 1968, p. 83.

2. We are indebted to Einstein and contemporary quantum physics for showing that energy, not matter, is the primal physical reality. Matter is energy in locked-up, informationally-structured form. Matter is fix-patterned energy.

3. Numerous well-known contemporary scientists consider awareness to be primal. John Eccles and Wilder Penfield saw mentality as primal but dualistic – an entity separate from energy/matter. Many others, including Gordon Globus, Bernard Rensch, Ervin Laszlo, Wolfgang Pauli, and George Wald have taken the position that mentality or awareness is, to use Wald's phrase, "intertwined and inseparable from the material universe." Globus calls this monistic perspective *double-aspect theory*, and says of it: "Double aspect theory holds that mind is but one aspect of a fundamental neutral reality with matter being the second aspect, both aspects having equal importance, as two sides of a coin."

   System theorist Ervin Laszlo contends that we are more justified to assume that subjectivity appears in all naturally-evolved systems than we are to assume that it appears only in humans and the higher animals. Laszlo, like Globus and Rensch, has advocated a two-perspective view of system functioning. In Laszlo's view, all natural systems have both an objective and a subjective nature, and the view of the system from each of these perspectives is quite different. When you look at a system from the outside you see a physical process. But each system also has an inherent subjective nature (however limited) and "sees," in some sense, to some degree, its own functioning from the inside. Even systems as simple as atoms presumably experience, to some extent, their own major events – such as an electron jumping from one orbit to another. Just as an atom embodies a tiny bit of energy it also embodies a tiny bit of awareness. It is an elemental mind as well as an elemental physical building block. The level of mind – its sophistication and the scope of its awareness – depends on the physical system's specific design, and secondarily, on its complexity. (See Penfield, *The Mystery of the Mind;* Eccles and Robinson, *The Wonder of Being Human;* Globus, "Mind, Structure, and Contradiction" in Globus, G., Maxwell, G., and Savodnik, I., eds. *Consciousness and the Brain: A Scientific and Philosophical Inquiry;* Rensch, *Biophilosophy;* Wald, "Cosmology of Life and Mind," in *Los Alamos Science: Fellows Colloquium,* Issue 16, 1988; Ervin Laszlo, *Introduction to Systems Philosophy.*)

4. A more complete discussion of this perspective appears in: Copthorne Macdonald, "An Energy/Awareness /Information Interpretation of Physical and Mental Reality," *ZYGON: The Journal of Religion and Science.* In press.

Chapter 2 – Emotion-Based Reactivity

5. A first-hand report of Paul D. MacLean's research into the limbic and reptilian brains can be found in "On the Evolution of Three Mentalities," in *New Dimensions in Psychiatry: A World View.* A book of MacLean's, now out of print except for an expensive photocopied version, is *A Triune Concept of Brain and Behaviour.* A book by another author that summarizes this and other research in the broad field of behavioural biology is Melvin Konner's *The Tangled Wing: Biological Constraints on the Human Spirit.*

6. For ethical reasons, the exploration of human brains has been much less drastic than the exploration of animal brains. Electrical stimulation and surgery have yielded some results, but most of our knowledge about human brain/mind and brain/behaviour interaction has come from naturally occurring brain tumours and lesions. Unusual behaviour, and personal accounts of unusual subjective experience, have been followed up after death by autopsies to determine which brain areas were affected.

7. This is Melvin Konner's assessment of Eleanor Maccoby's comprehensive reviews of the research in this area. (Melvin Konner, *The Tangled Wing: Biological Constraints on the Human Spirit*, New York: Holt, Rinehart and Winston, 1982, pp. 109-112.) The reviews themselves appear in Eleanor Maccoby and Carol Jacklin, *The Psychology of Sex Differences* and "Nurturance and Affiliation" in Eleanor Maccoby, Ed., *The Development of Sex Differences*.

8. Melvin Konner, *The Tangled Wing*, p. 121. Konner devotes chapter 6 of his book (pp. 106-126) to a sensitive exploration of this sometimes emotionally-charged issue: the extent to which male/female psychological differences are rooted in biology.

9. Melvin Konner, *The Tangled Wing*, p. 126.

Chapter 3 – Ignorance

10. If awareness was watching the direct output of the eye there would be a hole in the image. It would be like a TV system in which there's a defect in the camera tube; a spot appears in the video display. We don't see that retinal hole because awareness watches brain output, not eye output; the brain lies a little to awareness. The brain's sophisticated image processing creates an output in which that hole is filled in with conjured-up visual experience of the same subjective shade and brightness as nearby areas in the scene.

11. See Karl H. Pribram, "Problems Concerning the Structure of Consciousness" in Globus, G., Maxwell, G., and Savodnik, I., eds. *Consciousness and the Brain: A Scientific and Philosophical Inquiry*, New York: Plenum Press, 1976, pp. 304-306, and G. Bekesy, *Sensory Inhibition*.

12. This video analogy also points up the possibility that awareness itself need not move or zoom. It seems as though it does when we "turn our attention" from one thing to another. That same subjective effect, however, could be achieved with a fixed, constant awareness simply by adjusting the amplitude and "width" of the data flowing to it. Let's say that I'm reading a book and listening to music at the same time. What I perceive as turning my attention from listening to reading might just be the brain cranking up the amplitude of visual-field data, and simultaneously turning down the amplitude of hearing-field data.

Chapter 4 – Delusion

13. Quoted in Joseph Goldstein, *The Experience of Insight: A Natural Unfolding,* Unity Press, Santa Cruz, 1976, p. 126.

14. Ken Wilber has effectively pointed out that a Western therapy that attempts to build a strong ego and an Eastern practice that attempts to tear the ego down do not conflict if each is applied at the appropriate stage of growth. See his books *Spectrum of Consciousness,* and *No Boundary.*

15. See Arthur Koestler, *The Ghost in the Machine;* Eric Fromm, *The Anatomy of Human Destructiveness;* and the work of R. Paul Shaw and Yuwa Wong. (For example: R. Paul Shaw, "Humanity's Propensity for Warfare: A Sociobiological Perspective," *The Canadian Review of Sociology and Anthropology,* 22(2), 158-83, 1985.)

Chapter 5 – The Need for Wisdom

16. Rupert Sheldrake would also include *morphogenetic fields.* He has hypothesized that fundamental reality also includes informational fields created by previous occurrences of form in the universe. According to his theory, these fields extend throughout the universe and make the prior informational "habits" of the universe available everywhere to guide the present and future emergence of form and pattern. The hypothesis is testable in principle; to date, experimental results have been mixed. See Sheldrake's books *The Presence of the Past,* and *A New Science of Life.*

Chapter 6 – Dealing with Reactivity

17. See the Roger Sperry articles listed below for his view of the role of mind in this process:

    Sperry, R.W. "A Modified Concept of Consciousness." *Psychological Review*, 1969, Vol. 76, No. 6, pp. 532-536.

    Sperry, R.W. "Mental Phenomena as Causal Determinants in Brain Function," in Globus, G., Maxwell, G., and Savodnik, I., eds, *Consciousness and the Brain: A Scientific and Philosophical Inquiry*, New York: Plenum Press, 1976.

18. Two books that deal with the extent of culture's influence on us are anthropologist Edward T. Hall's book *Beyond Culture*, and the popular book by Joseph Chilton Pierce, *Exploring the Crack in the Cosmic Egg*.

19. Edward T. Hall, *Beyond Culture*, Garden City, NY: Anchor Press / Doubleday, 1976, p. 195.

Benjamin Libet's research is described in:

    Libet, Benjamin. "Unconscious cerebral initiative and the role of conscious will in voluntary action," *The Behavioural and Brain Sciences* 1985 8:4, 529-566.

    Libet, Benjamin. "Theory and evidence relating cerebral processes to conscious will," *The Behavioural and Brain Sciences* 1985 8:4, pp. 558-565.

Chapter 7 – Seeing the Unity: The Three Stages

20. Joseph Campbell, *The Hero with a Thousand Faces*, (Second Edition), Princeton: Princeton University Press, 1968, p. 167.

21. Alan Watts, *The Book: On the Taboo Against Knowing Who You Are*, New York: Vintage Press / Random House, 1972, p. 69.

22. This passage is from the book *I AM THAT*, a series of talks by Sri Nisargadatta Maharaj. Nisargadatta was a resident of Bombay and maker of handmade cigarettes. In his mid-thirties he had a Self-realization experience, and eventually became a Hindu saint. Some of the talks he gave when he reached his mid-seventies were recorded and translated by a Polish-born electrical engineer named Maurice

Frydman, a man whose own deep wisdom enabled him to capture the teachings in lucid and often luminous English. Nisargadatta was, during this latter period of his life, one of those who saw the unity all day, every day. He died in 1981 at the age of 84. (Nisargadatta Maharaj, Sri, Maurice Frydman, Tr., Sudhakar S. Dikshit, Ed., *I AM THAT: Conversations with Sri Nisargadatta Maharaj*, 3rd Edition, Durham, NC: Acorn Press, 1986, pp. 267-268.)

Chapter 9 – Seeing the Unity: Identifying with Being

23. Aldous Huxley, *The Perennial Philosophy*, p. 38 of the Chatto & Windus edition, London, 1969.

24. Nisargadatta Maharaj, Sri, Maurice Frydman, Tr., Sudhakar S. Dikshit, Ed., *I AM THAT: Conversations with Sri Nisargadatta Maharaj*, 3rd Edition, Durham, NC: Acorn Press, 1986, pp. 410, 413.

25. A directed lovingkindness meditation appears in Stephen Levine's book *A Gradual Awakening;* an audio cassette tape of this meditation is available from the Hanuman Foundation. See Chapter 14.

Chapter 10 – The Path to Wisdom

26. Several writers on intuition have commented on the conditions that facilitate this opening up of communication with the intuitive process. Tony Bastick in his book *Intuition: How We Think and Act.* (Chichester: John Wiley & Sons, 1982) said, "Intuition may be facilitated by increasing one's self-sensitivity using biofeedback and meditation" (p. 277). Virginia Burden Tower in *The Process of Intuition* (2nd Ed., Wheaton, Ill.: The Theosophical Publishing House, 1987) suggested that quiet messages from intuition occur "at times when you are very quiet and when desire and emotion have been stilled" (p. 83). Philip Goldberg in *The Intuitive Edge: Understanding Intuition and Applying It in Everyday Life* (Los Angeles: Jeremy P. Tarcher, 1983) said, "I agree with psychologist Frances Vaughan that 'the regular practice of meditation is the single most powerful means of increasing intuition'" (p. 179-180).

27. The decades mentioned are a rough indication of when these stages

typically occur in growth-motivated people. Maslow said that none of his self-actualizers was under 50, and Sam Keen in *Life Maps* puts the stage of the "childlike sage" late in life. It will be interesting to see if this pattern changes as more people in their 20s and 30s adopt spiritual practices.

28. If I'm ever tempted to doubt this I just have to recall those Buddhist monks I saw on television back in the early days of the Vietnam war. They had drenched themselves with gasoline, and sat cross-legged – still and silent – as they burned to death.

Chapter 11 – Freedom

29. Philip Goldberg, *The Intuitive Edge: Understanding Intuition and Applying It in Everyday Life*, Los Angeles: Jeremy P. Tarcher, 1983, p. 143.

Chapter 13 – A Wisdom-Based Culture

30. Joseph Campbell, *The Hero with a Thousand Faces*, (Second Edition), Princeton: Princeton University Press, 1968, pp. 388, 391.

Bibliography

Arguelles, Jose. *The Transformative Vision*. Berkeley: Shambhala Publications. 1975.

Assagioli, Roberto. *Psychosynthesis*. New York: Penguin Books. 1976.

Barnes, Hazel E. *An Existentialist Ethics*. New York: Alfred A. Knopf. 1967.

Barnes, Hazel. *Humanistic Existentialism*. (Out of print, but available in photocopy form from Books on Demand, University Microfilms, 300 N. Zeeb Rd., Ann Arbor, MI 48106.)

Barrow, J.D. and Silk, Joseph. "The Structure of the Early Universe". *Scientific American*. April 1980. pp. 118-128.

Barrow, John D., and Tipler, Frank J. *The Anthropic Cosmological Principle*. Oxford: Oxford University Press. 1988.

Bastick, Tony. *Intuition: How We Think and Act*. Chichester: John Wiley & Sons. 1982.

Bateson, Gregory. *Steps to an Ecology of Mind*. New York: Ballantine Books. 1975.

Bekesy, G. *Sensory Inhibition*. Princeton: Princeton University Press. 1967

Benedict, Ruth. *Patterns of Culture*. Boston: Houghton-Mifflin. 1961.

Bois, J. Samuel. *The Art of Awareness: A Textbook on General Semantics and Epistemics*, 3rd Ed. Dubuque: Wm. C. Brown. 1978.

Bridges, William. *Transitions: Making Sense of Life's Changes*. Reading, MA: Addison-Wesley. 1980.

Bucke, Richard M.D. *Cosmic Consciousness.* New York: E.P. Dutton.

Campbell, Jeremy. *Grammatical Man: Information, Entropy, Language, and Life.* New York: Simon and Schuster. 1982.

Campbell, Joseph. *The Hero with a Thousand Faces.* (Second Edition). Princeton: Princeton University Press. 1968.

Camus, Albert. *Notebooks 1935-1942.* New York: Modern Library.

Camus, Albert. *Notebooks 1942-1951.* New York: Alfred Knopf.

Carrington, Patricia. *Freedom in Meditation.* Kendall Park, NJ: Pace Education System. 1977.

Chomsky, Noam. *Language and Mind.* New York: Harcourt Brace Jovanovich. 1972.

Chomsky, Noam. *Modular Approaches to the Study of Mind.* San Diego: San Diego State University Press. 1983.

Da Free John. *Nirvanasara.* San Rafael, CA: Dawn Horse Press. 1982.

Da Free John. *The Bodily Location of Happiness.* San Rafael, CA: Dawn Horse Press. 1982.

Davies, Paul. *The Cosmic Blueprint: New Discoveries in Nature's Creative Ability to Order the Universe.* New York: Simon and Schuster. 1988.

Dawkins, Richard. *The Blind Watchmaker: Why the evidence of evolution reveals a universe without design.* New York: W.W. Norton. 1987.

de Ropp, Robert S. *The Master Game: Beyond the Drug Experience.* New York: Delacorte Press. 1968.

Durrell, Lawrence. *Justine.* New York: Pocket Books. 1961.

Durrell, Lawrence. *Balthazar.* New York: Pocket Books. 1961.

Durrell, Lawrence. *Mountolive.* New York: Pocket Books. 1961.

Durrell, Lawrence. *Clea.* New York: Pocket Books. 1961.

Eccles, John, and Robinson, Daniel N. *The Wonder of Being Human: Our Brain and Our Mind.* Boston: New Science Library. 1985.

Eliot, T.S. *Four Quartets.* London: Faber and Faber. 1959 (1944).

Field, Joanna. *A Life of One's Own.* Los Angeles: Jeremy P. Tarcher. 1981 (1936).

Fowler, Jim, and Keen, Sam. *Life Maps: Conversations on the Journey of Faith.* Waco, TX: Word Books. 1978.

Fromm, Eric. *The Anatomy of Human Destructiveness.* Greenwich, Conn.: Fawcett Publications. 1975.

Globus, Gordon G. "Consciousness and Brain I. The Identity Thesis" *Archives of General Psychiatry,* Vol. 29, Aug 1973, pp. 153-160.

Globus, Gordon G. "Mind, Structure, and Contradiction" in Globus, G., Maxwell, G., and Savodnik, I., eds. *Consciousness and the Brain: A Scientific and Philosophical Inquiry.* New York: Plenum Press. 1976.

Goldberg, Philip. *The Intuitive Edge: Understanding Intuition and Applying It in Everyday Life.* Los Angeles: Jeremy P. Tarcher. 1983.

Goldstein, Joseph. *The Experience of Insight: A Natural Unfolding.* Santa Cruz: Unity Press. 1976.

Goldstein, Joseph. *The Experience of Insight: A Simple and Direct Guide to Buddhist Meditation.* Boston: Shambhala Publications. 1983.

Goldstein, Joseph, and Kornfield, Jack. *Seeking the Heart of Wisdom: The Path of Insight Meditation.* Boston: Shambhala Publications. 1987.

Gould, Stephen Jay. *Time's Arrow Time's Cycle: Myth and Metaphor in the Discovery of Geological Time.* Cambridge, MA: Harvard University Press. 1987.

Gribbin, John. *In Search of the Big Bang: Quantum Physics and Cosmology.* New York: Bantam Books. 1986.

Griffin, Donald R. *Animal Thinking.* Cambridge: Harvard University Press, 1984.

Hall, Edward T. *Beyond Culture.* Garden City, NY: Anchor Press / Doubleday. 1976.

Hanh, Thich Nhat. *Peace is Every Step.* New York: Bantam Books. 1991.

Hanh, Thich Nhat. *The Miracle of Mindfulness.* Boston: Beacon Press. 1976.

Hawking, Stephen W. *A Brief History of Time: From the Big Bang to Black Holes.* New York: Bantam Books. 1988.

Hesse, Herman. *Demian.* New York: Harper and Row. 1965.

Hesse, Herman. *Siddhartha.* New York: New Directions Publishing Company. 1951.

Hoffman, Edward. *The Right to be Human: A Biography of Abraham Maslow.* Los Angeles: Jeremy P. Tarcher. 1988.

Huxley, Aldous. *The Perennial Philosophy.* New York: Harper and Row. 1970 (1946).

Ingram, Catherine. (Interview) "The Dalai Lama in Depth." *Yoga Journal,* Issue 90, Jan/Feb 1990, pp. 48-51, 85-87.

James, William. *The Varieties of Religious Experience.* New York: Mentor Books / New American Library.

Jaynes, Julian. *The Origin of Consciousness in the Breakdown of the Bicameral Mind.* Boston: Houghton-Mifflin. 1982.

Johnston, William, Ed. *The Cloud of Unknowing and The Book of Privy Counseling.* New York: Image Books / Doubleday. 1973.

Jones, Franklin. *The Knee of Listening.* San Rafael, CA: Dawn Horse Press. 1973.

Jung, C.G. *Analytical Psychology: Its Theory and Practice.* (The Tavistock Lectures delivered in London in 1935) New York: Vintage Books. 1968.

Kazantzakis, Nikos. *Report to Greco.* New York: Simon and Schuster. 1975

Kazantzakis, Nikos. *The Saviors of God.* New York: Simon and Schuster. 1960.

Kazantzakis, Nikos. *Zorba the Greek.* New York: Simon and Schuster. 1971

Keen, Sam. See Fowler, Jim and Keen, Sam.

Koestler, Arthur. *The Act of Creation.* New York: Dell Publishing Co. 1967, 1964.

Koestler, Arthur. *Janus: A Summing Up.* London: Hutchinson. 1978.

Koestler. Arthur. *The Ghost in the Machine.* London: Hutchison. 1967.

Konner, Melvin. *The Tangled Wing: Biological Constraints on the Human Spirit.* New York: Holt, Rinehart and Winston. 1982.

Krishnamurti, J. *The First and Last Freedom.* New York: Harper and Row. 1954.

Krishnamurti, J. *Commentaries on Living.* Wheaton, IL: Theosophical Publishing House. 1967 (1956).

Lao Tzu. *The Complete Works of Lao Tzu.* Los Angeles: College of Tao & Traditional Chinese Healing. 1979.

Lao Tzu. *Tao Te Ching.* Mitchell, Stephen. (Trans.) New York: Harper & Row. 1988.

Laszlo, Ervin. *Evolution: The Grand Synthesis.* Boston: Shambhala. 1987.

Laszlo, Ervin. *Introduction to Systems Philosophy: Toward a New Paradigm of Contemporary Thought.* New York: Gordon and Breach. 1972

Laszlo, Ervin. *The Systems View of the World.* New York: George Braziller. 1972.

Levine, Stephen. *A Gradual Awakening.* New York: Anchor Books / Doubleday. 1979.

Libet, Benjamin. "Unconscious cerebral initiative and the role of conscious will in voluntary action," *The Behavioral and Brain Sciences* 1985 8:4, 529-566.

Libet, Benjamin. "Theory and evidence relating cerebral processes to conscious will," *The Behavioral and Brain Sciences* 1985 8:4, pp. 558-565.

Maccoby, Eleanor, and Jacklin, Carol. *The Psychology of Sex Differences.* Stanford, Calif.: Stanford University Press. 1974.

Maccoby, Eleanor, ed. *Development of Sex Differences.* Stanford, Calif.: Stanford University Press. 1970.

Macdonald, Copthorne. "An Energy/Awareness/Information Interpretation of Physical and Mental Reality." *ZYGON: The Journal of Religion and Science.* In press.

MacLean, Paul. *A Triune Concept of Brain and Behavior.* (Out of print, but available in photocopy form from Books on Demand, University Microfilms, 300 N. Zeeb Rd., Ann Arbor, MI 48106).

MacLean, Paul. "On the Evolution of Three Mentalities." *New Dimensions in Psychiatry: A World View,* Vol. 2, edited by Dr. Silvano Arieti and Dr. Gerard Chzanowki. New York: John Wiley and Sons. 1977.

Maslow, Abraham. *Motivation and Personality.* New York: Harper and Row. 1970.

Maslow, Abraham. *Toward a Psychology of Being,* 2nd Ed. New York: Van Nostrand Reinhold. 1968.

Maslow, Abraham. *The Farther Reaches of Human Nature.* New York: Penguin Books. 1976.

Maslow, Abraham. *Religions, Values, and Peak Experiences*. New York: Viking Press. 1970.

Maxwell, Grover C. Maxwell's remarks in Globus, G., Maxwell, G., and Savodnik, I., eds. *Consciousness and the Brain: A Scientific and Philosophical Inquiry.* New York: Plenum Press. 1976.

Meadows, Donella et al. *The Limits to Growth*. London: Earth Island Limited. 1972.

Milner, Marion — see Field, Joanna

Monod, Jacques. *Chance and Necessity.* New York: Random House / Vintage Books. 1972.

Nisargadatta Maharaj, Sri. Maurice Frydman, Tr. Sudhakar S. Dikshit, Ed. *I AM THAT: Conversations with Sri Nisargadatta Maharaj*, 3rd Edition. Durham, NC: Acorn Press. 1986.

The Open Focus Handbook. Princeton: Biofeedback Computers, Inc. 1982.

Ornstein, Robert, and Thompson, Richard F. *The Amazing Brain*. Boston: Houghton-Mifflin. 1984.

Ornstein, Robert. *The Psychology of Consciousness*, Second Edition. New York: Harcourt Brace Jovanovich. 1977 (First Edition, 1972).

Pagels, Heinz R. *The Cosmic Code: Quantum Physics as the Language of Nature*. New York: Bantam Books. 1983.

Penfield, Wilder. *The Mystery of the Mind: A Critical Study of Consciousness and the Human Brain*. Princeton: Princeton University Press. 1975.

Piaget, J. *The Child's Conception of the World.* Paterson, New Jersey: Littlefield Adams and Company. 1960.

Pierce, Joseph Chilton. *Exploring the Crack in the Cosmic Egg*. New York: Pocket Books. 1974.

Popper, Karl R., and Eccles, John C. *The Self and Its Brain*. New York: Springer-Verlag. 1977.

Prebble, John. *Glencoe: The Story of the Massacre*. London: Secker and Warburg. 1966.

Pribram, Karl H. "Problems Concerning the Structure of Consciousness" in Globus, G., Maxwell, G., and Savodnik, I., eds. *Consciousness and the Brain: A Scientific and Philosophical Inquiry.* New York: Plenum Press. 1976.

Rensch, Bernard. *Biophilosophy.* New York: Columbia University Press. 1971.

Rexroth, Kenneth. "William Golding." *The Atlantic Monthly.* Volume 215, No. 5, May, 1965.

Rilke, Ranier Maria. *Letters to a Young Poet,* Revised Edition. Tr. by M. D. Herter Norton. New York: W.W. Norton. 1954.

Sartre, Jean Paul. *Being and Nothingness.* New York: Philosophical Library. 1956.

Sartre, Jean Paul. *Existentialism and Human Emotions.* New York: Philosophical Library. 1947.

Schumacher, E.F. *A Guide for the Perplexed.* New York: Harper and Row. 1977.

Shaw, R. Paul, and Wong, Yuwa. "Humanity's Propensity for Warfare: A Sociobiological Perspective." *The Canadian Review of Sociology and Anthropology,* 22(2): 158-83. 1985.

Sheehy, Gail. *Passages.* New York: Bantam Books. 1977.

Sheldrake, Rupert. *A New Science of Life: The Hypothesis of Formative Causation.* London: Blond and Briggs. 1981.

Sheldrake, Rupert. *The Presence of the Past: Morphic Resonance and the Habits of Nature.* New York: Times Books. 1988.

Sperry, R.W. "A Modified Concept of Consciousness." *Psychological Review,* 1969, Vol. 76, No. 6, pp. 532-536.

Sperry, R.W. "Mental Phenomena as Causal Determinants in Brain Function." in Globus, G., Maxwell, G., and Savodnik, I., eds. *Consciousness and the Brain: A Scientific and Philosophical Inquiry.* New York: Plenum Press. 1976.

Sperry, Roger. *Science and Moral Priority: Merging Mind, Brain, and Human Values.* New York: Columbia University Press. 1983

Spitz, R.A. "The smiling response: a contribution to the ontogenesis of social relations." *Genet. Psychol. Monogr.* 34, 57-125, 1946.

Suzuki, D.T. *The Manual of Zen Buddhism.* New York: Grove Press. 1960.

Tower, Virginia Burden. *The Process of Intuition,* 2nd Ed. Wheaton, Ill.: The Theosophical Publishing House. 1987.

Trungpa Rimpoche, Chogyam. *Cutting Through Spiritual Materialism.* Boston: Shambhala Publications. 1973.

Trungpa Rimpoche, Chogyam. *Shambhala: The Sacred Path of the Warrior.* Boston: Shambhala Publications. 1984.

Wald, George. "Cosmology of Life and Mind." *Los Alamos Science: Fellows Colloquium,* Issue 16, 1988.

Watts, Alan. *The Book: On the Taboo Against Knowing Who You Are.* New York: Vintage Press / Random House. 1972.

Watts, Alan. *The Meaning of Happiness: The Quest for Freedom of the Spirit in Modern Psychology and the Wisdom of the East.* New York: Harper Colophon Books. 1969 (1940).

Weinberg, Gerald. *An Introduction to General Systems Theory.* New York: Wiley. 1975.

Weinberg, Stephen. *The First Three Minutes: A Modern View of the Origin of the Universe.* Updated Edition. New York: Basic Books. 1977, 1988.

Wilber, Ken. *No Boundary: Eastern and Western Approaches to Personal Growth.* Boston: Shambhala Publications. 1981.

Wilber, Ken. *The Spectrum of Consciousness.* Wheaton, IL: Theosophical Publishing House. 1977.

Wilber, Ken. *Up From Eden: A Transpersonal View of Human* Evolution. Boston: Shambhala Publications. 1983.

Wilhelm, R. and Baynes, C.F. translators. *The I Ching: or Book of Changes.* Princeton, NJ: Princeton University Press. 1967.

Wright, Robert. *Three Scientists and Their Gods: Looking for Meaning in an Age of Information.* New York: Times Books. 1988.

Glossary

Terms as they are used in *Toward Wisdom*

acceptance
A non-reactive mental stance in which no attempt is made to avoid, or escape from, the informational reality present at this moment. (Acceptance does not, however, imply that things should necessarily remain as they are, and that nothing should be done to make the future different from the present. One simply recognizes that reacting emotionally to what already *is* serves no purpose.)

Advaita Vedanta
A branch of the Vedanta school of Hindu philosophy which holds that only a three-aspect Ultimate Principle (Brahman) exists, and that phenomenal existence (maya) is an illusion. Brahman's three aspects are:

Being (sat) – which I take to be energy, the primal medium,

Subjective awareness or consciousness (chit),

and

Bliss or primal happiness (ananda).

algorithm
A general specification of the way that things must happen. In computer programming an algorithm is the list of data manipulations that will ulti-

mately be coded in some computer language. In brain programming it is the definition of the way that information will be processed by the brain when that program is "running." In nature it is the set of rules that determine how physical reality will function: the *laws* of nature.

analog
An informational structure in one medium that parallels (at least to some degree) a second informational structure – usually in another medium.

analogy
A mode or way of knowing based upon the inherent parallelism of analogs.

ancient-brain
Pertaining to the fixed-programmed reptilian and limbic parts of the human brain.

archetype
A fundamental, often-repeated informational pattern. In particular, the term refers to the universal themes, myths, images, and other informational structures which apparently come hardwired into each brain – a key part of what Carl Jung called the "collective unconscious."

Atman
In Hindu philosophy the true Self, pure awareness, the subjective aspect of Brahman.

attention
Directed awareness.

Awareness
The aspect of the cosmic medium that underlies and makes possible the subjective, mental world. The subjective aspect of reality. The subjective function. The contentless ground of mind which, when modulated by informational patterns, becomes mind itself, becomes awareness with informational content.

Being
That which is. The real. The eternal. Energy-Awareness.

Big Bang
The event approximately 15 billion years ago which marked the beginning of our present expanding universe, the establishment of space and time, and the start of the evolutionary process.

bliss
See **happiness (fundamental)**.

Brahman
In Hindu philosophy, the Ultimate Reality or Ultimate Principle. Brahman has three aspects or attributes which are:

Being (sat) – which I take to be energy, the physical aspect of the primal medium,

Subjective awareness or consciousness (chit),

and

Bliss or primal happiness (ananda).

chance
The fortuitous, unaccountable, and for practical purposes, unpredictable element in existence. Included here are not only those events which are thought to be intrinsically random (such as quantum-level events) but also those "mechanical" events that are uncontrollable and thus unpredictable, and those events which result from the convergence of two or more independent chains of cause and effect.

computer
An information processing system with information inputs, information outputs, information memory, and program-controlled manipulation of input and memory data to produce the output data.

concept
A mental model of some aspect of reality; often a general relationship that is characteristic of a certain class of specific instances.

consensus reality
The accepted view of reality within a particular culture – the view which most people have, the view inculcated and reinforced by cultural institutions.

data
In the broadest sense, information. More commonly, data is information that was, is, or will be recorded, transmitted, or processed in some manner.

ego
The state of local self-interest created whenever the primal sense of identity becomes linked with the body, with intellectual activity, or with reactive emotion.

emotions (reactive)
A group of intense and generally unpleasant mental/physical states which arise in reaction to various informational stimuli. They are forms of wanting what you don't have (desire, greed, lust, envy, jealousy, etc.) and wanting to get rid of what you do have (loneliness, anger, hate, fear, disgust, etc.).

emotions of being
Subtle emotional colorations (low-level mind contents) that often accompany the quiet-mind experience of Being. Among them are peace, equanimity, quiet joy, happiness at the good fortune of others, wonder, compassion, a sense of energy, etc.

Energy
The medium that underlies and makes possible the objective, physical world. The E of Einstein's equation: $E=mc^2$. The contentless ground of the physical world which, when modulated by (or arranged in) informational patterns, becomes the various "forms" of matter and energy.

equanimity
Freedom from the restless need to act, to do, to change what is going on in the present moment.

evolution
The process by which the universe – from the Big Bang to its final state – acquires its overlay of increasingly intricate informational patterns.

existence
The realm of phenomena, in which eternal Being (Energy-Awareness) is formed or modulated by changing informational patterns.

existential
Pertaining to existence.

experiential knowing
A deep level of knowing in which intellectual models and intuitive insights have become profoundly internalized. Here, one's experience is in accord with the internalized framework. There may be a direct sense of oneness, for example. Or the present moment may be experienced as a time-free and spacious NOW, without the usual sense that now is an elusive instant between a vast past and a vast future.

form
The modulations, or patterns of significant difference, produced when a medium undergoes modulation.

gestalt
A pattern or other informational complexity perceived as a whole. (A pattern of lines on paper perceived as a person's face, for example.)

gestalt flip
A psychological phenomenon in which the pattern of data currently giving rise to one perceived whole or gestalt suddenly gives rise to a new whole, a new gestalt. (Gestalt flips occur when viewing "ambiguous" drawings, and are characteristic of many "flashes of insight.")

ground of being
The primary medium, energy-awareness, which is modulated by informational patterns to create the realm of physical/mental phenomena we call existence.

happiness (fundamental), bliss

Our basic or root mental state. Awareness colored with contentment and equanimity. Awareness accompanied by a feeling that everything is basically OK. Awareness, either free from all forms of wanting (all reactive emotions), or utterly detached from them. Happiness is primal, noumenal, fundamental, whereas both pleasure and unhappiness are informational.

hard-wired

Those parts of any data-processing system (human or computer) which cannot be changed at all, or cannot be changed without drastic physical intervention.

hardware

In a data-processing system, the physical structures which support and enable the processing.

holistic seeing

A non-needy being-grounded whole-system sort of perception in which a wide range of data is taken in and processed without the distortion and filtering that is characteristic of needy, personal, goal-oriented perception.

identification

A mental process in which the primal sense of existing becomes associated with specific mind content or the external reality which that mind content represents.

identity delusion

The delusion, almost universal among human beings, that our true identity is that of person, and person only. It occurs when the primal sense of existing becomes identified with the body, and with the brain's emotional and intellectual activity. It vanishes when the misidentification dissolves, and when awareness is seen to be the true home of this sense.

imperturbability (place of)

A mental state which – despite the presence of potentially distressing mind content – is characterized by inner stillness, freedom from emotional reactivity, and lack of identification with the show going on in consciousness.

information
Patterns of significant difference which modulate, wave, or shape various primary or derivative media and are in some sense "carried" by them. (See the more complete discussion in Chapter 1.)

insight meditation
A form of attention training in which awareness of bodily activities and mind contents is used to develop increased continuity of attention, and insight into the nature of the mind/body process. (It is a Buddhist practice, also called *Vipassana* and *mindfulness* meditation.)

insights
Newly acquired perspectives on what *is*, new ways of looking at things, new gestalts abstracted from the available data.

intellectual knowing
Knowing through informational analogy. A mode of understanding in which a mental model or concept in some sense parallels aspects of a real-world situation.

intelligence
Using internalized information and values to guide a response to newly-encountered information. (This definition applies to human intelligence, to intelligence in artificial systems, and to the intrinsic intelligence of the cosmic process.)

interest
Intense and focused awareness. Awareness with all the help a body/mind can give it.

intuition
A largely unconscious but holistic information processing activity carried on by the brain. The information inputs to this process appear to include sensory experience, previously arrived at concepts and mental models,

and genetically-inherited archetypal material. Informational outputs include insights, hunches, premonitions, warnings, and commands to act. Intuitive process programs include creative problem solving, and helping the individual deal effectively and wisely with life situations.

intuitive knowing

Broadly, any knowledge acquired through the intuitive process. While often not as detailed and explicit as intellectual knowing, intuitive knowing tends to be more deeply believed – one is more likely to base life decisions on it. While it sometimes involves intellectual concepts and images, intuitive knowing often takes simple forms such as hunches, and *yes* or *no* feelings. At times it is knowing by identification – knowing by being the thing known.

knowledge

Interpreted information, information in perspective. Information seen through, or in relationship to, an interpretive framework of some kind. See **intellectual knowing, intuitive knowing,** and **experiential knowing.**

laws of nature

Verbal and mathematical expressions of the recursive algorithms which underlie the individual subprograms of the overall program which determines how nature works and evolution progresses.

liberation (spiritual)

Freedom from domination by reactive emotion, by compulsions of all types (including compulsions to use the intellect), by identification with the body/mind, and by other mind content that does not reflect wisdom.

limbic brain

See limbic system.

limbic system

The middle portion of the human brain, both physically, and in terms of its evolutionary origin. It is the old mammalian brain which surrounds the still older reptilian brain, and is in turn surrounded by the more recently evolved neocortex. Included within its structure are the thalamus, hypothalamus, amygdala, pituitary, and hippocampus. It is a key part of the brain circuits which generate reactive emotions and behavior.

love
As subjective process, love is interest and acceptance. As objective process, love is that proactive movement in which Being-values become manifested in the informational show of existence.

meditation
In the context of this book, various exercises designed to train attention and quiet the mind. This sort of meditation involves:

1. Choosing an appropriate place to put attention,
2. Training it to stay there, and in some cases
3. Developing a more inclusive, wider-angle mode of attending.

medium
That which carries, supports, or is modulated by an informational pattern or message.

mental model
A subjective informational construct, created by the brain, and organized in ways which parallel (to some extent) the informational organization of objective existence.

message
An informational pattern which modulates, or is carried by, a medium.

metaphor
One informational construct which stands for, or represents, another.

micro-culture
A person's life situation looked at as though it were a culture – paying particular attention to the influences to which that situation regularly subjects the person.

mind
A subjective emergent of brain system functioning in which awareness is modulated by informational patterns, and which exerts a top-down influ-

ence on the systems and subsystems which give rise to it. (Identical or very close to Roger Sperry's view. See his articles listed in the Bibliography.)

mind content
Those informational patterns which comprise subjective experience.

Mind-essence
The Zen term for the ground of mind. (What I call pure, unmodulated awareness.)

mindfulness
Clear awareness of what is happening here and now. Awareness of mind contents, the body, and the immediate situation.

mindfulness meditation
See **insight meditation.**

modulation
The process of impressing an informational pattern on a medium. Also, the pattern itself, as conveyed by the medium.

morphogenetic fields
As hypothesized by biologist Rupert Sheldrake, they are fields, present throughout the universe, which guide the development of informational structures, and are themselves "strengthened" by the presence of such structures in other places.

necessity
Jacques Monod's term for the rigid determinism which dictates what will happen next in a given physical situation because nature operates according to unchanging laws.

neocortex
The outer layer of the brain (the new brain or "roof brain") in which human intellectual activity takes place.

Nirvana
As I use the term, the medium of existence independent of any informational modulation. The ground of mind that underlies content: pure awareness.

noumenon
The informationless ground of being. Energy-Awareness.

noumenal
Residing or inhering in the primal ground of being, in the eternal cosmic medium.

noumenal creativity
Love in action. That proactive movement in which noumenal values (the high values of Being) become manifested in the informational structures of the phenomenal world. It is wisdom-based creativity, as contrasted with reactive or "problem solving" creativity.

personal self
The ego. The self-experience when identification with the body and/or mind contents is present.

perspective
An interpretive framework through which raw data or factual information is related to a context. An interpretive framework through which information becomes personal knowledge.

We have four primary modes of knowing: instinctive/ reactive, perceptual, intellectual, and intuitive. In each mode the term *perspective* has its own distinct meaning because the four modes employ altogether different interpretive frameworks. In the instinctive/reactive mode of knowing, the interpretive framework consists of a palette of *reactive emotions*. In the perceptual mode of knowing, there are several frameworks: *physical location*, *memories* of other perceptions, and the *gestalt or figure/ground or whole/part effect*. In the intellectual mode the interpretive frameworks include *concepts, mental models, theories, paradigms*, and *symbol systems* such as *language*. In the intuitive mode the interpretive frameworks are *feeling-ordered* and include *identification* and *conviction*. Shifts in figure/ground, whole/part gestalts occur in the intuitive mode too, but they not perceptual gestalts, they are intuitive gestalts related to being and existence. They are ways of "seeing" or coming to grips with certain fundamental aspects of what *is*.

phenomena
Aspects of existence involving both medium and message. Physical phenomena involve energy and various informational overlays – various forms or modulations of that energy. Mental phenomena involve awareness and brain-produced modulations of awareness.

pleasure
A frequently sought, transient state of mind – the attainment of which is the object of much human activity. It arises in response or reaction to certain perceptions, and to the recognition of certain informational patterns. See also **happiness.**

program
The set of rules and procedures which guides and directs an information processing activity.

quiet mind
A mind in which little or no discursive thought, reactive emotion, or identification with mind content is present. What is present is awareness, various sense perceptions, and perhaps one or more of the subtle "emotions of being".

reactivity
The body/mind's tendency to react to circumstances with stereotyped reptilian- and limbic-brain responses such as anger, envy, fear, jealousy, greed, possessiveness, concern about status, territoriality, etc. See also **emotions (reactive).**

reptilian brain
The innermost part of the human brain – the *corpus striatum* and related structures – which is our evolutionary inheritance from the reptiles. It is thought to play a role in territoriality, the establishment of social hierarchies, ritualized behavior, and aggression.

ripening
A metaphor in which spiritual practice is seen as a process which helps a person gradually "ripen", or slowly move toward the moment when the fruit of insight and self-realization suddenly drops.

Samsara

Existence, or the phenomenal world: Energy overlaid with information. Awareness with informational content.

self (spelled with a small s)

Identity associated with the body, with intellectual activity, or with reactive emotion. The personal self, the ego. That mental state which the *identity delusion* creates.

Self (spelled with a capital S)

Pure subjective awareness, the ground of perception and mind. Also, Energy-Awareness: the ground of being.

self-actualization

Abraham Maslow's term for the state of full psychological development, creative functioning, and fulfillment. The motivation to attain self-actualization normally arises after an individual's deficiency needs (physiological, security, relationship, and esteem needs) have been largely met.

Self-realization

The understanding, at a deeply intuitive and experiential level, that the true "self" is not the human body/mind but is the permanent medium or *Ground of Being* which interpenetrates the informational universe, supports it, and enables it to exist.

space-time

The four-dimensional framework or matrix within which physical phenomena occur.

Spirit

Energy-Awareness. The universal medium. The Ground of Being which interpenetrates the informational universe, supports it, and enables it to exist.

spiritual

Having to do with primal realities, and the human recognition of those realities.

spiritual practice
A set of procedures intended to help the participant recognize primal truths and to act in accord with their implications.

stillness
A subjective state characterized by attentiveness, equanimity, and freedom from identification with, or reaction to, mind contents. In this state all movement, all change, is perceived as external, as other, as part of the observed information.

subjectivity
Awareness. Receptivity. The ground of perception and mind.

surrender
An attitude of non-reactivity and greatly diminished ego in which the conscious intellectual process accepts what *is* at this moment, and is ready to be guided by intuitive wisdom into the next.

system
A patterned whole involving interacting and interdependent components in which some basic set of relationships among those components is maintained.

system (artificial)
Systems designed in detail by human beings, and built by them. Examples are television sets, computers, and railroads.

system (natural)
Systems that are not the result of conscious human planning. Included among these are atoms, molecules, cells, organs, plants, animals, ecosystems, clans, communities, etc.

Tao
The Source of all things. The Ground of Being. The fundamental medium of existence: Energy-Awareness.

unhappiness, displeasure
The disturbance of primal happiness caused by wanting the present situation to be different.

values
The algorithm-like ability to lead toward specific kinds of consequences. Built-in preferences. And Ervin Laszlo's definition: "Goals which behavior strives to realize."

Vipassana meditation
See **insight meditation.**

wisdom
A mode of living in which holistic values and the intuitive process (rather than reactive ancient-brain programming or the culture-based programming of the rational mind) exercise primary control over one's behavior and inner experience. In wisdom, the intellect may aid and augment, but does not exert primary control. Among wisdom's values are upleveling the process and enhancing the well-being of the whole. (See Chapter 1 for a more complete discussion.)

wisdom-based culture
A culture in which the attainment of wisdom by all members is a central value.

wrong view
The Buddhist label for identification with body and mind contents.

Index

Printed in the USA
CPSIA information can be obtained
at www.ICGtesting.com
JSHW082205140824
68134JS00014B/445

9 780888 821515